SURVIVAL PENDING REVOLUTION

SURVIVAL PENDING REVOLUTION

The History of the Black Panther Party

PAUL ALKEBULAN

The University of Alabama Press
Tuscaloosa

Typeface: Garamond

∞

The paper on which this book is printed meets the minimum requirements of American
National Standard for Information Sciences-Permanence of Paper for Printed Library
Materials, ANSI Z39.48–1984.

Library of Congress Cataloging-in-Publication Data

Alkebulan, Paul.
Survival pending revolution : the history of the Black Panther Party / Paul Alkebulan.
p.   cm.
Includes bibliographical references and index.
ISBN-13: 978-0-8173-1549-8 (cloth : alk. paper)
ISBN-10: 0-8173-1549-7
1. Black Panther Party—History. 2. Revolutionaries—United States—History—20th
century. 3. Radicalism—United States—History—20th century. 4. African Americans—
Politics and government—20th century. 5. African Americans—Civil rights—History—
20th century. 6. United States—Race relations—Political aspects—History—20th
century. 7. Black Panther Party—Biography. I. Title.
E185.615.A627 2007
322.4′20973—dc22

2006038430

This book is dedicated to the rank and file of the Black Panther Party who worked and sacrificed, often anonymously, to implement their community programs: medical clinics, liberation schools, and free breakfasts for schoolchildren. Their courage and devotion was in the best tradition of the African American struggle for democracy.

CONTENTS

ACKNOWLEDGMENTS

I want to take this opportunity to thank the people and institutions that assisted in this project. This book would not have been possible without the wholehearted cooperation of the many former Panther Party members who graciously consented to be interviewed over the years. I knew some of these men and women from 1969 through 1971. There were others, however, who I met for the first time in the course of my research. They were always courteous and cooperative. Their candor inspired my work.

Archival research in Panther material was conducted courtesy of the Moorland-Spingarn Research Center, Howard University, and the Department of Special Collections, Stanford University Libraries. Their staff members were always professional, helpful, and patient with my numerous requests.

INTRODUCTION

> In 1966 we called ourselves a Black Nationalist Party because we thought
> that nationhood was the answer....Shortly after that we decided that what
> was really needed was revolutionary nationalism, that is, nationalism plus
> socialism. After analyzing conditions a little more we found...we had to
> unite with the peoples of the world so we called ourselves Internationalists.
> ...But then...we found that everything is in a state of transformation....
> These transformations...require us to call ourselves "intercommunalists"
> because nations have been transformed into communities of the world.
>   —Huey P. Newton, November 1970

Huey Newton and Bobby Seale founded the Black Panther Party (BPP) in October 1966 at the beginning of the Black Power movement. The Panther Party
existed for sixteen years as one of the most controversial political organizations
in American history. The BPP's career was marked by heated revolutionary
rhetoric, social service programs, international diplomacy, clashes with the police, and internal conflicts.

Opinions formed forty years ago about the BPP still exist today. The party's
critics have vilified it as a loosely organized group of criminal anarchists with
political pretensions. Panther supporters, on the other hand, have argued that
the party was a community service organization undermined by the government because FBI director J. Edgar Hoover opposed the very thought of black
people having civil rights.

Political and historical reality, however, refuses to adhere to these simplis-
tic positions. Many individuals and organizations, for instance, supported the
Panthers on some issues and criticized them on others. Party members also
could and did decide that some activities were worth supporting, whereas other
policies resulted in resignations. In other words, people and politics evolve and
change over time, principle, or convenience.

Some historians might believe that it is too early for a proper assessment of the BPP. For instance, some former members may be hesitant, for one reason or another, to discuss all their activities or those of their friends. On the other hand, the government may be reluctant to reveal all the information in their possession about the activities of their agents provocateurs. I am not certain, however, whether the immediate future will bring about more openness in these areas.

I believe that good work can be done now. BPP veterans are all around us. In addition, Panther Party records are available in public archives and private collections. Historians have begun to ask many questions. For example, what exactly was the BPP's ideology? What did it hope to accomplish? What were the reasons for the major ideological shifts in party history? What was the impact of basing organizing efforts on "the brothers on the block"? What role did women play? And, finally, whom did the BPP appeal to and why?

Comprehensive academic studies of the BPP began in 1978 with Charles Hopkins's Ph.D. dissertation titled "The Deradicalization of the Black Panther Party: 1966–1973." Angela Ernest-LeBlanc (formerly Darlean Brown), Kathleen Cleaver, Kit Kim Holder, Tracye Matthews, and Robyn Spencer have all written theses or dissertations on the BPP in the last fifteen years. Their works are either comprehensive national histories or studies of the role of women and international diplomacy in the BPP.

I am confident that these works are only the beginning of a new wave of scholarship on the BPP and black militancy during the twentieth century. Specialized regional studies of the chapters or the activities of the party's artists and musicians, for instance, can and should be part of the new wave of scholarship.

I have not attempted to chronicle the activities of every state chapter, local branch, or National Committee to Combat Fascism. I have chosen a different task. *Survival Pending Revolution* will discuss the BPP's appeal, what the members hoped to accomplish, what they actually achieved, the obstacles they encountered, and their legacy. This text will extend BPP historiography by demonstrating that party history can be divided into three different ideological eras. Each era had a different political objective. This approach will help to explain the varying political tendencies the Panthers displayed from 1966 to 1982.

The three eras are 1966 to 1971, 1971 to 1974, and 1974 to 1982. Different social circumstances, political philosophies, and activities characterized each era. Each time frame is further distinguished by a declension of ethical and political standards among the leadership that increasingly drove many dedicated members from the organization.

From 1966 to 1971 the Panthers were self-proclaimed revolutionaries advocating political autonomy for black America. Although never completely abandoning that stance, the BPP also embraced other ideologies, such as socialism, Marxism, and its own unique vision of a new world order: intercommunalism.

The party's advocacy of community control of police, education, politics, and economics attracted thousands of recruits as it expanded beyond Oakland to sixty-one cities across the United States.[2] Meanwhile, in 1969 exiled Panthers under the leadership of Eldridge Cleaver, minister of information, established an international section in Algeria.

The BPP also began community service activities in 1969. These activities were the free breakfast programs for schoolchildren, liberation schools, and free medical clinics. The efforts were intended to address the immediate needs of the black community. The Panthers also hoped to use these programs to provide positive activities for the rank and file and to educate the community toward a revolutionary understanding of the American political system.

Their ultimate goal at this time was to change that system to a socialist entity.[3] The programs were popular within the party and the community, but some Panthers believed they diverted the organization from its primary responsibility of leading an armed rebellion against the government.[4]

Meanwhile, the U.S. government had begun a counterintelligence program in 1967 (known as Cointelpro) to eliminate black radicals and negate their influence.[5] The Panther Party was not one of Cointelpro's initial targets. Soon, however, the BPP became the prime focus of government efforts because it was outspoken about the need for armed struggle to influence political change. Cointelpro campaigns against the Panthers resulted in the deaths of several members and the arrest of hundreds. These attacks strained organizational resources to the limits.

The government campaign also affected the party's leader, Huey Newton. Newton had been arrested in 1967 and convicted of manslaughter a year later for killing a policeman in an early morning shootout. Newton was released from jail in 1970 when his conviction was overturned on appeal. The events of the previous three years had changed Newton's political perspective. He had begun to doubt that armed struggle could be successful.

Newton was therefore reluctant to continue the militant tactics that had gained the Panthers their initial reputation as revolutionaries. By January 1971 he had openly eschewed armed struggle and threw his weight behind using community programs to organize the black community.[6]

Party militants believed Newton's about-face had betrayed them. They had made tremendous sacrifices because of his earlier words and actions. Their disaffection resulted in a direct challenge to Newton's leadership in 1971. The challenge resulted in a factional split, with a loss of life on both sides. The confl ostensibly revolved around which was the best way to lead the black community toward political change. Should the BPP educate the community through the community service programs or through a campaign of armed propaganda designed to ignite a socialist revolution?

In reality, the Panthers also fell victim to a sophisticated counterintelligence operation designed to manipulate existing internal conflicts (and instigate others) among leaders and the rank and file. Each side of the schism claimed to be the "real Black Panther Party," but the faction aligned with Huey Newton prevailed. The community service programs continued and became the party mainstay. The party's first ideological era ended in 1971 with a disengagement from armed confrontation with the government.

The Panthers continued their survival programs from 1971 to 1974 during the second ideological era. They were also involved in electoral politics when Bobby Seale and the new minister of information, Elaine Brown, ran for Oakland's mayor and city council, respectively. The BPP closed many offices across the country and redirected resources to Oakland in a massive effort to win the election.

This strategy proved to be an error because some members left the organization rather than carry out what they believed was an incorrect policy of shutting down viable local programs to concentrate on what were essentially Oakland electoral politics.[7] The subsequent defeat of Bobby Seale and Elaine Brown disillusioned some of the remaining members. If the BPP could not win in its birthplace, what chance did it have to recoup its fortunes in other regions?

While Seale was being defeated, Newton and his inner circle were engaged in drug use and physical violence against party members and the community. They also misappropriated organization funds for their personal use.[8] Ethical questions came to a head in 1974 when Newton had to flee to Cuba after being accused of murdering a prostitute.

These developments led to further membership losses. One of the legacies of this period was the party's growing negative perception in the black community. This perception conflicted with the self-image and self-respect of rank-and-file members. The result was a further drain of talented and dedicated people.

Party leadership devolved to Elaine Brown in Newton's absence, and she tried to improve the party's image by involvement in city government through the Panther's Oakland community school and membership on various city commissions. The 1974 to 1982 period was also the era when women increasingly occupied leadership roles. JoNina Abron became editor of the newspaper in 1978. Erika Huggins and Brenda Bay were the directors of the Oakland Community School, and women dominated the personnel makeup of the community programs.

Newton returned in 1977 to stand trial for the murder of a prostitute, and his presence once again focused negative publicity on the BPP. This was due to his increasingly erratic behavior that culminated in the botched murder attempt of one of the witnesses in his murder trial.[9] This trial and a later one resulted in hung juries. Meanwhile, Newton wrested control of the party from Brown, and she subsequently resigned after a hasty nocturnal flight to Los Angeles.[10]

The Panther newspaper ceased publication in 1980, and the official demise of the party occurred in 1982 when the Huey P. Newton Educational Institute (formerly the Oakland Community School) closed its doors. The third era was over, and the BPP was history.

Survival Pending Revolution is organized thematically. The introduction and prologue provide some background information for the newcomer to Panther history. Chapter 1 will examine how and why the BPP's ideology changed over time. There I will also discuss how the Panther Party's beliefs influenced its relations with political organizations, students, and businesspeople.

Chapter 2 explores the Panther Party's rationale for beginning its community action programs. The community programs are perhaps the BPP's most well-known legacy. It is important to understand their origin, function, successes, and shortcomings.

Chapter 3 discusses some of the party's regional offices. I have chosen representative chapters from California, the Pacific Northwest, the Midwest, the South, Algiers, and the East Coast. In my opinion their stories illustrate the issues faced by the BPP as it developed from a small, local group to an international organization with a diplomatic mission in Africa.

Chapter 4 covers the questions of revolutionary violence, dissent within the party, and how the U.S. government's counterintelligence program subverted the BPP. This chapter also examines why the BPP initiated its own underground organization and how this connection eventually proved to be a two-edged sword. Chapter 4 will also occasionally refer to the political events of the previous chapters. Chapter 5 reviews the complex and important role women played in the Panther Party. Chapter 6 narrates the BPP's decline, and the epilogue discusses the party's multifaceted legacy.

I have also supplied a bibliographic essay that discusses the significant works and archival resources on the Black Panther Party. I hope this resource will encourage other historians to delve into the party documents, government memos, and news articles that are open to the public.

I have attempted to avoid the false dichotomy of portraying the Panther Party as a selfless community service organization or a group of criminal anarchists with political pretensions. The truth is far more complex because the party displayed many sides during its sixteen-year existence. The challenge is to understand why. In order to do this, we must begin with the circumstances that gave birth to the Black Panther Party.

ABBREVIATIONS

BLA	Black Liberation Army
BPP	Black Panther Party
CIA	Central Intelligence Agency
COINTELPRO	Counter-Intelligence Program
CORE	Congress of Racial Equality
FBI	Federal Bureau of Investigation
LCFO	Lowndes County Freedom Organization
NAACP	National Association for the Advancement of Colored People
NCCF	National Committee to Combat Fascism
NLF	National Liberation Front (South Vietnam)
NOI	Nation of Islam
OAAU	Organization of Afro-American Unity
OCS	Oakland Community School
PE	Political education
PPII	People's Party II
RPCC	Revolutionary Peoples Constitutional Convention
SCLC	Southern Christian Leadership Conference
SDS	Students for a Democratic Society
SNCC	Student Nonviolent Coordinating Committee
SSAC	Soul Students Advisory Council
YLP	Young Lords Party
YPP	Young Patriot Party

SURVIVAL PENDING REVOLUTION

PROLOGUE

When black people send a representative he is somewhat absurd because he
represents no political power. He does not represent land power because we
do not own any land. He does not represent economic or industrial power
because black people do not own the means of production. The only way
he can become political is to represent what is commonly called a military
power.

— Huey P. Newton, February 1970

The post–World War II American civil rights movement united disparate
political and economic groups in a struggle for democratic rights and social
change. Individuals and organizations, black and white, formed a united front
to overturn *Plessy v. Ferguson* and end the legal disfranchisement and physical
terror endured by millions of African American citizens. The common cause
elided political, social, and philosophical differences among allies as diverse as
the National Association for the Advancement of Colored People (NAACP),
the Southern Christian Leadership Conference (SCLC), the Student Nonviolent Coordinating Committee (SNCC), the Americans for Democratic Action,
the AFL-CIO, the Urban League, the Congress of Racial Equality (CORE),
and, occasionally, the U.S. government.

Civil rights organizations and African American religious, fraternal, and
civic groups were primarily interested in the defeat of legal and social barriers
to full participation in the American mainstream. The U.S. government, on
the other hand, saw the civil rights movement primarily through a cold-war
prism. This prism defined the "Negro problem" as a public relations issue that
must be solved or managed for the benefit of American foreign policy. Consequently, segregation and the disfranchisement of millions of citizens were seen

as glaring errors in American society that hindered the government's portrayal of itself as a champion of democracy in Africa, Asia, and Latin America.[1]

Mainstream African American organizations, mindful of the domestic anti-Communist climate and because of their own beliefs, were careful not to challenge the democratic and free market consensus that prevailed in the United States. Consequently, critiques of capitalism were avoided for the most part. Civil rights leaders preferred to concentrate on making America live up to its promise of "freedom for all" regardless of race, creed, or color.

The movement's leaders reasoned that to achieve this goal it was first necessary to secure civil rights for African Americans as a *group*. Only then would it be possible for *individual* blacks to take advantage of their skills and education to integrate into mainstream America.

The efficacy of this tactical decision seemed to be borne out by the Supreme Court's *Brown v. Board of Education* decision. Furthermore, the 1963 March on Washington, the 1964 Civil Rights Act, the 1965 Voting Rights Act, and the subsequent Great Society legislation were great victories for the civil rights movement. The worldview of moderate blacks and whites was apparently validated by the liberal promise of color-blind advancement in public and private arenas.

Not all African Americans were content with this political stance, however. The 1964 Harlem and 1965 Watts riots alerted the nation to new areas of racial discontent. Southern blacks had moved north and west during the great migration and World War II in search of the social justice and economic improvement that had eluded them in their birthplaces. Instead of the land of milk and honey, they found a prejudiced legal system, inferior education, employment discrimination, and slum housing.

The civil rights movement's main emphasis was initially on voting and equal access to public accommodations. This *seemed* distant from ghetto concerns with police brutality, jobs, and housing. In addition, some black activists were concerned with the so-called national question. In other words, what was the exact nature of black Americans' relationship to the U.S. government?

W. E. B. DuBois had argued that historically there were two schools of thought or organized programs on this issue.[2] The first program argued for ceaseless agitation to achieve political rights, as well as civic and social equality. In this view blacks were citizens who had been denied their constitutional rights to equal protection of the law. The NAACP's legal strategy and the

SCLC's mass protests were intended to force the majority population and the government to redress African American grievances.

DuBois referred to the second school of thought as the "back to Africa" program. Marcus Garvey and the Universal Negro Improvement Association epitomized this ideal. The "back to Africa" idea, however, can be traced to a 1788 proposal by Philadelphia's Free African Society, Paul Cuffe's 1815 voyage to Sierra Leone, and the founding of Liberia. Outrage over the Compromise of 1850 and the Supreme Court's 1857 Dred Scott decision reignited the movement. There was also an internal migration scheme after the Civil War that advocated homesteading on the Great Plains. This was fueled by dissatisfaction with the subordinate political and economic status of blacks after the war.

A subset of the first school was the idea that self-segregation and economic nationalism should precede political activism in order to smooth the path to full civil rights. Booker T. Washington, founder and president of the Tuskegee Institute from 1881 to 1915, was one of the most notable exponents of this school of thought. The strategic goal of both philosophies was the achievement of full citizenship for African Americans. The debate, therefore, was over means, not ends.

DuBois also conceived of a third path to obtain full equality and civil rights by arguing that blacks should utilize a partially segregated economy to fund their own education, health, legal, and housing initiatives. DuBois believed this tactic would enable blacks to enter mainstream America on the best possible terms because a greater degree of economic self-sufficiency could bolster their political status.[3]

Some critics might point out that this third program was actually the reviving of Washington's ideology years after his death. This is a good point. It is enough, however, to acknowledge that both men believed that economic prowess was a viable means to help achieve the goal of full citizenship.

The social and political ferment created by the successful civil rights movement after World War II and the rise of national liberation movements in Africa, Asia, and Latin America enhanced the emotional and ideological appeal of nationalism among young blacks. They defined nationalism as achieving political and economic control over the black community.[4] Many of these young people (both in and out of the civil rights movement) were frustrated with the apparently slow pace of black advancement. The Nation of Islam was especially outspoken about achieving freedom from white control.[5]

Minister Malcolm X, after being expelled from the Nation of Islam, began to articulate a political agenda that closely identified the African American struggle for human rights with anticolonial wars in Africa and Asia. He believed this tactic would enhance the domestic human rights struggle. Malcolm's brilliant and searing rhetoric was very influential among the younger generation of civil rights activists. Consequently, the desire of young black radicals for *internal* political and economic autonomy radically transformed DuBois' concept of the second historical school.

These were some of the social and ideological conditions that existed in October 1966 when Huey Newton and Bobby Seale founded the Black Panther Party (BPP). The Newton and Seale families were part of the black migration out of the South to a better life on the West Coast. There were no unique attributes that distinguished Newton or Seale from other working-class black youth with similar backgrounds. They were indifferent students, and both had brushes with authority. Seale was discharged from the air force after a run-in with his commanding officer. Newton was occasionally incarcerated because of petty criminal activities.[6]

Like other young blacks of the civil rights era, they were searching for answers to America's seemingly intractable racial problems. They were unable to articulate completely their own belief system. Nevertheless, they did not believe that intellectuals or middle-class blacks had much to offer the African American poor. They were also uninterested in nonviolent resistance. They were attracted, however, to Malcolm X's clarion call to freedom "by any means necessary."[7]

Furthermore, their life experiences up to this point had persuaded them to identify with the "brothers on the block." These were the small-time criminals and the unemployed and underemployed men of the community. These individuals were precisely the sorts of men who would be likely to have problems with most authority, black or white.[8]

Newton and Seale attended Merritt College in Oakland during the 1960s, where they became members of an organization called the Soul Students Advisory Council (SSAC). The SSAC wanted to establish a black studies program. The college administration resisted the move. Newton and Seale attempted to persuade the SSAC to wear arms at a rally as a way to persuade the administration to accede to their educational demands. They also wanted to move the student group to adopt armed self-defense as a political program for the survival of black people. Both men saw the police force as government-sponsored brutality. The students resisted because they failed to see the reason for resorting to arms in an educational environment.[9]

Newton and Seale, meanwhile, had also begun studying the works of Malcolm X, Robert F. Williams, the West Indian psychiatrist Frantz Fanon, and the Argentinean revolutionary Che Guevara. The net result of their research was to convince Newton and Seale that the black community was under attack by the government.

They formed the BPP in October 1966 to end police brutality. The two men began with armed patrols to monitor the police in the black community. Newton and Seale carried law books and shotguns as they conducted their surveillance. The idea was to inform blacks of their legal rights and prevent police misconduct. The police naturally objected to their presence because they believed their safety and authority were undermined. They were right because the Panthers were very clear that they intended to do just that.[10] The Panthers also adopted a ten-point program that called for the following:

1. The freedom to determine the destiny of the black community.
2. Full employment for blacks.
3. An end to the robbery by the white man of the black community ("white man" changed to "capitalist" by 1969).
4. Decent housing for blacks.
5. A relevant education for blacks.
6. Exemption from all military service for blacks. (In 1972 this was changed to a demand for free health care.)
7. An immediate end to police brutality against blacks.
8. Freedom for all black men held in federal, state, county, and city prisons. (In 1972 this was changed to a demand for the end of all wars of aggression.)
9. Black defendants to be tried only by a jury of fellow blacks. (In 1972 this was combined with the demand for freedom for all black prisoners so it would be one issue.)
10. A UN-supervised plebiscite to determine the will of black people as to their national destiny.[11]

In May 1967 the Panthers carried out an armed demonstration in Sacramento to protest pending passage of the Mulford Act. The proposed legislation would outlaw the carrying of loaded firearms in public. Newton and Seale believed the law would inhibit the ability of blacks to defend their community from potential government oppression. Several Panthers were arrested in the Sacramento protest and sentenced to jail terms.[12]

Police-Panther tensions reached a boiling point when Newton was arrested in October 1967 for the murder of a policeman following a late-night traf stop in Oakland. The BPP responded by organizing the Free Huey movement to save Newton from the death penalty. The Free Huey movement grew from a local group to an international organization that spread party news and ideology across the globe.

An Oakland-based BPP central committee was also established. Its members were either friends or known to each other. The principal officers were as follows: Huey Newton, minister of defense; Bobby Seale, chairman; Eldridge Cleaver, minister of information; David Hilliard, chief of staff; Kathleen Cleaver, communications secretary; and Emory Douglas, minister of culture. Various individuals held the education and finance portfolios during the party's existence. When the BPP expanded across the country, state chapters replicated the national structure, with deputy ministers and deputy chairmen responsible for organizing in their own areas. State chapters were subordinate to national headquarters in Oakland and subject to its orders.[13] The Panther Party began as part of the modern Black Nationalist movement. The movement was frustrated by the inability of civil rights laws to address effectively the issues of police brutality, structural unemployment, inferior schools, slum housing, a biased justice system, and political impotence for blacks in urban America.

In 1966, however, the Panthers were only one of a number of groups in the Black Nationalist community. They were not even the best known. The public was more familiar with the Student Nonviolent Coordinating Committee (SNCC) under the leadership of Stokely Carmichael and H. Rap Brown. SNCC had a long record of voting rights activism in the South.

SNCC had formed the Lowndes Country Freedom Organization (LCFO) in Alabama that used a panther as their symbol. SNCC intended the LCFO to be the forerunner of similar political organizations throughout the country. SNCC began to call for "Black Power" in 1966. This slogan was defined as full participation in all the decision-making processes that affected African Americans.[14]

Public attention started to focus on the Panthers soon after they began police patrols and demonstrated in Sacramento. Newton's arrest and the birth of the Free Huey movement propelled the Panthers into the national spotlight. That light shined brighter when they laid claim to Malcolm X's mantle.

I

THE HEIRS OF MALCOLM

It is the wisdom, the strength, and the love for humanity that was Malcolm
that was the motivating force in the founding of the Black Panther Party.
—*Black Panther,* May 1969

Malcolm X was the ideological patron saint of the Black Panther Party. It was
Malcolm who articulated the party members' doubts about the political af-
filiations and integrationist orthodoxy of the civil rights establishment. It was
Malcolm who provided them with new definitions for politics, race, and self-
esteem that were capable of transforming ordinary people into committed activists. It was Malcolm who journeyed to Africa to rekindle lost ties with a
new generation of political leaders. Last, it was Malcolm who persuaded some
young blacks to believe they should pick up the gun and defend themselves
from what they viewed as state oppression.

Malcolm symbolized the individual's capacity for spiritual and mental rejuvenation through self-discipline and active involvement in the civil rights
movement. This was especially true because he had overcome drug use and a
prison record. His example inspired those from similar backgrounds. Panthers
knew that Malcolm's story was in many respects their story as well.

Malcolm X influenced the BPP through four primary beliefs: (1) that African Americans could use arms to achieve political aims; (2) that individuals
could achieve spiritual and mental rejuvenation through participation in the
movement; (3) that blacks should be open to alliances with other ethnic groups
but only on a basis of mutual self-respect; and (4) that the civil rights move-

ment was part of an international struggle against racism and Western capitalism.

This last belief was very complex. On the one hand, it could be utilized to draw spiritual strength for the domestic civil rights movement. This would be in keeping with DuBois' belief that African Americans had a double consciousness. They were American and "Negro." Blacks were not only distinctly American but paradoxically also separate and unique. DuBois argued that blacks wanted to integrate without losing their cultural uniqueness.[1] On the other hand, it could also be used to define American blacks as a domestic colony that could be justified in calling for political independence from the United States.

Malcolm X (born Malcolm Little) had endured a childhood of poverty after the death of his father and subsequent mental breakdown of his mother. Malcolm gravitated to the streets of Boston and New York and became a small-time hustler before being convicted for burglary in 1946. He underwent a spiritual conversion in prison and joined Elijah Muhammad's Nation of Islam (NOI) in 1948.

Malcolm became a Muslim minister after his release. His hard work propelled him to the status of a trusted aide to Elijah Muhammad. Malcolm was expelled from the organization in March 1964 for questioning Elijah Muhammad's personal ethics. He also chafed under the NOI's noninvolvement policy in the civil rights struggle. Malcolm believed that the Muslims should defend civil rights workers in the South.

He founded the Organization of Afro-American Unity (OAAU) after his expulsion from the NOI. Malcolm claimed that Black Nationalism was his political philosophy, which he defined as blacks controlling the politics and economy of their community to improve material and spiritual conditions. He attributed the social ills of blacks to white racism, a lack of control by blacks over their own affairs, and the allegedly misguided politics of an "integrationist minded" black elite.[2]

Malcolm believed school and housing integration were unrealistic goals for average blacks because whites could successfully resist these attempts by simply moving away. Consequently, blacks would be the majority in most of the communities where they lived. Integration was a chimera if you accepted Malcolm's argument. Self-help was the only option. In other words it was necessary for blacks to be responsible for their own social and political destiny.

Malcolm argued that the nationalist philosophy would "wake up" blacks to their plight and that, once aroused, they would defend themselves against those who sought to abuse them. Malcolm urged his followers to analyze the national liberation struggles in Africa and Asia where independence was obtained through armed struggle. He sought the support of the Organization of African Unity for the American civil rights struggle. Malcolm also attempted to persuade the United Nations to investigate domestic abuse of African Americans.

Malcolm was assassinated in February 1965, and several members of the Nation of Islam were later convicted of the crime. His death was viewed as a great tragedy by many young blacks. They had accepted the Muslim minister as a new type of leader who wanted to broaden the horizons of the civil rights movement by linking it with independence struggles in Africa and Asia. Malcolm and these activists reasoned that linking civil rights with national independence struggles would radically transform the domestic character of the civil rights movement into a revolutionary international human rights struggle.

The American civil rights movement was clearly part of the worldwide struggle for democracy, modernization, and national liberation in the mid-twentieth century. The civil rights movement was able to forge sometimes-tenuous political alliances across racial and ideological barriers. Within the black community the alliance meant that nationalists and integrationists agreed on the need for fundamental civil and political rights.

The nationalists, however, also articulated a message of political autonomy. Thus, the civil rights movement began to assume a dual character. The dominant integrationist ideology defined the struggle as a movement to secure full citizenship rights through legal agitation and mass mobilization. The smaller but extremely vocal nationalist faction encompassed a broad spectrum of individuals and groups struggling for goals ranging from full autonomy to increased political and economic control over the African American community.

The Black Panther Party was initially a radical nationalist movement calling for political autonomy. A significant part of BPP ideology was based on Malcolm X's vision of transforming domestic civil rights struggles into a revolutionary movement through alliances with third-world governments and national liberation movements. BPP central committee member Landon Williams recalled, "We felt ourselves to be the heirs to Malcolm, and I remember Malcolm saying, 'We demand to be treated as a man and a human being in this society right now, and we will have it by any means necessary.' It still makes the hair stand up on the back of my neck to hear it or to say it because I still believe it."[4]

The Use of Arms to Achieve Political Aims

The first aspect of Malcolm's influence was the area of self-defense or the use of arms to achieve political goals. The 1964 Harlem and 1965 Watts riots were armed uprisings against police brutality and the lack of economic opportunity. These urban rebellions convinced the BPP and other militant nationalists that blacks were engaged in a struggle for political independence from the United States. The Panthers moved quickly to call for armed struggle and identification with third-world liberation movements.

Even after the death of Dr. Martin Luther King, however, urban rebellions did not produce a revolutionary tidal wave around America. Radical groups did, of course, organize. Nevertheless, the widespread destruction in long-established black communities also had a sobering effect on the majority of more moderate (or realistic) blacks. Their moderation helped to channel political dissent into electoral politics. This option was an opportunity to achieve goals peacefully within the existing political system.

Malcolm never gave a definitive answer as to whether arms were to be employed strictly in self-defense or as part of a broader strategy to achieve political autonomy. The lack of clarity reflected uncertainty as to whether blacks were an internal American colony (which presumably meant recourse to an armed struggle) or citizens struggling for long-denied legal rights. If blacks were engaged in a legal struggle to obtain constitutional rights, then a resort to arms would be a dubious proposition. The obvious caveat would be in cases of self-defense.

The example of Robert F. Williams would be an instance on how self-defense tactics could have unintended consequences. Williams had been president of the Monroe, North Carolina, chapter of the NAACP. Like many Southern communities, Monroe had been subject to racist terror attacks. Williams had formed an NAACP rifle club to defend the black community against violence from the Ku Klux Klan. The club successfully repelled an armed Klan motorcade in October 1957.[5]

In May 1959, Williams was a courtroom observer when two white men were acquitted of assault against black women. An angry Williams stated: "We must be willing to kill if necessary. We cannot take these people who do us injustice to the court and it becomes necessary to punish them ourselves. In the future we are going to have to try and convict these people on the spot.... We get no justice under the present system.... If it's necessary to stop lynching with lynching, then we must be willing to resort to that method."[6]

Williams was suspended from the NAACP for his statements. His suspension, however, did not change the highly charged atmosphere in North Carolina. Monroe was the scene of intense racial disturbances in July and August 1961. A series of arsons targeted white and black businesses. Freedom Riders demonstrated against segregation. There were also more armed confrontations between blacks and whites.[7]

During one of these incidents a white couple was driving through the black community. Some of the residents thought the car had been seen earlier, carrying a racist banner. The vehicle was surrounded, and the couple was forced to take shelter in Williams's house before being released. Williams was accused of kidnapping, and a warrant was issued for his arrest. He fled to Cuba to avoid the charges.[8]

Williams's supporters applauded him for attempting to defend the community from mob violence. They also attacked the kidnapping charges as a trumped-up prosecution to rid North Carolina of a bold and dedicated civil rights activist.

Williams's activities, however, raised several interesting questions. When and how were arms to be employed in self-defense? Who was to do it? What training should they have? What political groundwork was necessary to prepare public opinion? How do you prepare for the government's inevitable negative reaction? Should you assume government agents would try to infiltrate your ranks?

None of these questions were fully discussed or solved by the nationalist wing of the civil rights movement. At least they were not discussed in public. From December 1963 to February 1965, Malcolm was involved in legal and doctrinal disputes with the NOI, made two overseas trips, gave many speeches throughout the United States, attempted to organize the OAAU, and tried to provide for his family. Not surprisingly, he had little opportunity to provide the public with a practical working demonstration of his platform before he was assassinated.

The ambiguities during Malcolm X's last months did not stop the BPP from claiming what it believed to be his legacy. The party published annual tributes to his life from 1967 through 1971. These epistles discussed international relations, armed struggle, and why blacks should control their community's affairs.[9]

The BPP praised Malcolm for clarifying the Southern and Northern experiences to blacks. They contended that Malcolm showed there was no substantive difference between Northern and Southern racism. The Southern experience was more easily understood because of its blatant racism. The subtler but equally effective tactics of political gerrymandering and community redlining characterized the Northern experience. The Panthers maintained that Malcolm was owed a debt of gratitude for his contribution. They argued that blacks could pay the debt by engaging in a revolutionary struggle for self-determination.[10]

Spiritual and Mental Rejuvenation

The second aspect Malcolm influenced was the idea of renewal through struggle. Many young blacks, in a manner typical of youth, were looking to infuse their lives with purpose. Carrying on in the footsteps of Malcolm was portrayed as a worthy endeavor. These messages were powerful recruiting tools for the Panthers, and they found a willing audience amid the turmoil of the 1960s. Youth throughout the country rallied to the party banner as "freedom fighters." Articles filled the pages of the *Black Panther* in 1968 that called for blacks to fulfill their "revolutionary duty."[11]

Bobby Seale and Huey Newton also studied Mao Zedong and Frantz Fanon. Mao was recognized as a leader of a national liberation movement and as someone who had stood up to American power in Asia.[12] Fanon was a psychiatrist from the French West Indies and a World War II veteran. He had joined the Algerian National Liberation Front during Algeria's struggle for independence.

Fanon argued that revolutionary violence would rehabilitate the personality of oppressed people as well as liberate their countries. Embracing violence would allow the dispossessed to recover their human dignity through the struggle because they had nothing to lose and everything to gain.[13] Newton and Seale accepted Fanon's arguments and incorporated them into Malcolm dictum that blacks should defend themselves against mistreatment and protect their political rights by any means necessary.

The Panthers also believed that African Americans were an internal colony of the United States and were fighting for national liberation. They urged sympathetic whites to assist them by staging a revolution in the larger society.[14] The Panthers believed they were carrying Malcolm's arguments to their logical conclusion by adopting this colonial analogy. The Panthers thus justified their political position in the classic terms of a national liberation struggle.

Newton and Seale agreed with Malcolm and Fanon's assertion that the underclass was capable of being redeemed through revolutionary action. This was significant because the party's founders were convinced their young organization should be based on this social group.[15] Newton and Seale argued that these men were the most fearless members of the community because of their frequent encounters with the police.

Other activists disagreed with this formulation, however. Writer Earl Ofari argued that the BPP leadership failed to recognize that the majority of blacks were workers. Ofari maintained that any successful social movement (revolutionary or not) should start with workers and their concerns, that is, jobs, education for their children, dignity, and quality of life. The party's leadership consciously made the black underclass the focus of their organizing efforts. Ofari did not believe the underclass was capable of generating "enough internal discipline and cohesion to organize a structure capable of providing leadership for the black community."[16]

Ofari noted that the problem with the underclass was that one could never be sure of the group's loyalty. Like the black elite they were capable of being "revolutionary" one day and working in some government-funded community program the next day. Their "ideological" positions tended to be based on immediate advantage or emotionalism.[17]

Ofari believed this decision could inhibit the intellectual and political growth of the BPP because the underclass would prove to be incapable of successfully building the long-term intergroup alliances that would ground them firmly in the most productive part of the African American community. As it would turn out, redemption for individual members of the underclass would be more probable than redemption for a whole social class.

The first issue of the BPP newspaper maintained that whites had instilled fear into blacks to keep them from organizing to achieve their legal rights. The police were described as an occupying army in the black community that enforced the larger society's illegitimate rule. The BPP believed the only way to remove the black communities' fear was to confront the police with arms.[18]

There was, however, a contradiction between the party's means and ends. None of the BPP's original ten-point program and platform was revolutionary in the sense that it demanded a change of government.

The Panthers did demand self-determination. This was interpreted in a variety of ways, however, ranging from a UN-supervised plebiscite to electing blacks to public office. With the exceptions of the provisions on the draft and the plebiscite, the program was not markedly different from what other community organizations had been demanding. In fact, it bore a startling resemblance to the Nation of Islam's platform.[19]

Consequently, the BPP put itself in the paradoxical position of initially making reformist demands and threatening to implement them with revolutionary means (guns). Furthermore, the Panthers were not just exercising their free-speech rights when they demanded an end to police brutality. From 1966 to 1971 Panthers believed they should "establish revolutionary political power" through armed struggle.[20]

Newton wrote that the vanguard party, that is, the BPP, should attack policemen in small groups to instruct blacks in the "correct strategic means of resistance" against what the Panthers called an occupying force in the community.[21] Newton also wrote that the party could make a tremendous impact and inspire similar actions through these tactics before it was driven underground. Confrontations with the government, however, were costly to the BPP and resulted in Newton being arrested for murder in 1967.

David Hilliard claimed the Panthers ambushed three policemen in a Hunters Point housing office in November 1967 and killed one of them.[22] In 1968 Eldridge Cleaver, David Hilliard, Bobby Hutton, and seven other Panthers attempted to ambush Oakland police officers. The attack ended with Hutton dead, Cleaver wounded, and the other eight under arrest. At the time, the party claimed the police had attacked the members while they were gathering barbecue supplies for a political rally the following day. In 1993, however, David Hilliard conceded that the affair was a Panther ambush.[23]

Some of the BPP's supporters have criticized the group for allowing military confrontations to define its image during the late 1960s. They argue that this was a serious tactical error because the party's political choices were limited due to decisions made at its founding. The critics have also argued that the Panthers never completely realized that though small groups might stage small armed attacks, only a politically conscious and aroused community could implement a "victorious people's war."[24]

This argument has some merit, but the criticism is only partly true. Although shootouts received more headlines, the Panther Party realized that guerilla tactics were only one aspect in a struggle for political independence. In fact, it also used other strategies, such as political and interracial alliances.

Alliances with Other Ethnic Groups

The third aspect Malcolm influenced was the idea of alliances with other ethnic groups if there were common interests and mutual respect. Malcolm X said that he broke with the NOI's doctrine of black racial supremacy after his pilgrimage to Mecca because he was exposed to the more-inclusive message of universal brotherhood. The pilgrimage encouraged Malcolm to believe that not all whites were inherently evil. He pronounced himself ready to work for social change with white allies on a basis of mutual respect.[25]

The Panthers implemented Malcolm's idea of making interracial alliances for specific purposes by forming an electoral coalition with the Peace and Freedom Party in 1968.

Peace and Freedom was a mainly white, middle-class organization of Vietnam War protestors who had endorsed the Panther ten-point program and platform.

The Panthers used the alliance to publicize their program. They also declared that black politicians would lose votes if they failed to work for Newton's freedom. Peace and Freedom, on the other hand, hoped to broaden its base and acquire black votes through the Panther alliance.[26]

In 1968 the coalition ran Eldridge Cleaver for president, Dr. Benjamin Spock for vice president, along with Huey Newton for Congress and Bobby Seale and Kathleen Cleaver for state assembly.[27] Ultimately, however, most blacks voted Democratic in 1968, but the alliance did raise funds for Newton. It also had the benefit of setting a precedent for future alliances with Hispanics and other whites.

The BPP worked with white and other ethnic organizations on an as-needed

basis. The party sometimes solicited support for Panther prisoners or simply issued joint statements praising each other's political positions and urging solidarity in the struggle against the prevailing American political structure. The
main point is that unlike the NOI or other nationalist organizations, the BPP
had no qualms about making coalitions with other ethnic groups whenever it
suited its political purposes.[28]

In 1969 the Chicago branch of the BPP would form a "rainbow coalition"
with the Puerto Rican Young Lords Party (YLP) and the white Young Patriots
Party (YPP). The YLP had been a Puerto Rican gang based in Chicago. The
Panther Party's influence helped to transform the YLP into a political organization working for Puerto Rican independence. The YPP was an organization
of young whites working for social change in the white community.[29]

By 1969 the BPP leadership believed that black self-determination was impossible without a wide-ranging political and social revolution that included
all of the American people. The party's survival demanded that it reach out to
potential allies who could support it in its increasingly dangerous struggle with
the U.S. government. The BPP began to move away from Black Nationalism
to socialism and class struggle.

The BPP maintained that a major contradiction existed between the black
community and capitalism. Panthers believed that only socialism and communal ownership of the means of production could provide the economic conditions for the self-determination of black people. The BPP called this position
revolutionary nationalism, which it defined as nationalism plus socialism.[30]

The Panther Party argued that one of the reasons the United States became
an industrial power was because of the tremendous profits realized through domestic slavery's superexploitation of blacks. The Panthers said that blacks had
remained in a subordinate position after slavery because they lacked adequate
political and economic power.

The Panther Party began discussing class divisions in the black community
in a very rudimentary fashion by utilizing the stock characters of the supposedly favored house Negro versus the field Negro. Malcolm X often used these
mythological figures as a rhetorical device to attack the civil rights establishment. The field Negro was recast as a working-class or marginally employed
black. The house Negro was alleged to be a middle-class professional or politi-
cian who benefited financially by betraying the interests of the masses.[31]

Panthers claimed to represent the implacable and rebellious nature of the field Negroes who were impatient with the black middle class's leadership. Kathleen Cleaver illustrated the point in 1968 by asserting that black lawyers had not responded to Huey Newton's legal plight. She went on to claim that most of the civil rights lawyers she was familiar with in the South were whites and that black lawyers were only concerned with economic security and not the success of the movement.[32] Regardless of the accuracy of her statement, Charles Garry and other white lawyers did represent Newton and the Panthers in a wide variety of legal matters.

The Panthers also initially maintained that black businesspeople exploited the community just as whites did. The Panthers acknowledged that despite this criticism, many African Americans had a general reluctance to condemn black capitalism because they perceived it as a legitimate attempt to control the community's economy for the general good. Many blacks also believed that due to racism, they had a close relationship regardless of class or position.[33]

The BPP changed its position in 1971 and began to say it was possible for black businesspeople to work for national liberation through making contributions to Panther community programs. In return the Panthers would stop their criticism and advertise friendly businesses in their paper.[34] Although this position had a certain crass self-interest, it did allow the party to conciliate a potential ally. It also had the additional benefit of maintaining the BPP's self-proclaimed position as the sole arbiter of revolutionary ideology in the black community.[35]

This position was critical in its struggle with black cultural nationalists. Panthers defined cultural nationalists as those who wanted to return to the African past through dress, language, or religion. According to the Panthers, these individuals believed that regaining a cultural identity was either a prerequisite to obtaining political freedom or an end within itself.[36] The BPP claimed that even though identification with African heritage was necessary, mere surface appearances alone would not liberate black people.

The Panthers argued that only a revolutionary culture was worthwhile because revolution meant a change in the political condition of black people. In addition, the Panther Party claimed that guerilla movements struggling for national liberation represented the true culture of Africans.[37]

The Panthers believed that culture was a dynamic and constantly changing phenomenon that should not be obsessed with artifacts from a preindustrial past. This stance brought the Panthers into conflict with such prominent cultural nationalists as Ron Karenga. Karenga was the leader of the Los Angeles–based US organization that competed with the BPP for power and influence among other African American groups.[38]

The cultural nationalists in turn accused the Panthers of importing a foreign ideology (Marxism) into the black community and becoming the willing tools of white communists. These hostile political disputes allowed the government to instigate bloodshed between both organizations in 1969. (A more complete discussion of the Panther-U.S. problem is presented in chapter 4.)

Panther politics also ended a 1968 merger with the Student Nonviolent Coordinating Committee. Newton wanted to incorporate SNCC leadership into the BPP to provide the Panthers with much-needed administrative experience and a recognizable national leadership. SNCC hoped to benefit from the party's appeal with grassroots urban dwellers. The SNCC alliance ultimately failed, however, because of differences in organizational histories, constituencies, ideologies, and leadership.

SNCC's constituency was in the Southern civil rights movement, and the Panthers at the time were a Northern and Western urban organization. Stokely Carmichael, James Forman, and Rap Brown were more experienced organizers and leaders than Newton and Seale. Therefore, Carmichael may have expected the Panthers to bow to his leadership, but they refused to do so. There were also personality clashes. The SNCC leaders claimed they were physically threatened by the BPP, and the alliance fell apart by early 1969.[39]

The Panthers also attempted to build alliances with student groups. Point number five of the Panther ten-point program called for education that would teach blacks to achieve their true role in American society as revolutionaries. As noted earlier, Newton and Seale began their political careers as activists with the Soul Students Advisory Council at Oakland's Merritt College. The SSAC's initial activities were focused on ending the draft of black men and beginning a black studies program. A fundamental contradiction soon emerged between the future Panthers and other students.

Newton and Seale wanted to leave the campus and organize in the black community, preferably with guns. The other SSAC leaders wanted to confine their activities to campus issues. The Panthers referred to these students as "cultural nationalists" because they saw student issues as separate from larger political issues.[40]

This political dispute pointed out a very real problem for the Panthers. The

BPP was so convinced of its ideological correctness that it insisted on dominating the decision-making process in any alliance. This stance could create a great deal of resentment among potential allies. Problems usually centered on demands that students unconditionally support all Panther policies.

Some black students were reluctant to submit to party leadership because they did not want to be mere political appendages. Alliances were more successful when there were mutual interests, such as black studies departments or the continuous campaigns to free Panther prisoners.

Still, the BPP did manage to work successfully with African American high school and college students to organize curriculums and black student unions. A 1968 statewide conference convened in California to discuss a national organization of black students. Attendees developed a ten-point program for students that was similar to the Panther program.[41] The national student organization never reached fruition, but the BPP continued to work with high school students on a local level.

Colleges and universities also became a prime recruitment area. In California the Panthers targeted San Francisco State University, the University of California–Los Angeles, Merritt College, and other schools for organizing efforts. George Murray, a San Francisco State student, was the party's minister of education during the winter of 1968–69. He led a strike by the San Francisco State black student union to force the college administration to grant demands for a black studies department. This strike set a precedent for other black students throughout the nation. It would encourage them to pursue African American studies aggressively on their own campuses.

Murray and other activists were arrested and sentenced to jail terms, but their efforts led to a black studies department. In 1968 Merritt College students were able to begin an African American Studies Department without a strike. According to the student activists, the purpose of these departments was to offer an interdisciplinary curriculum in the humanities or social sciences concerning problems of African Americans in the larger society and the contributions of Africans or African Americans to American culture. The departments would award degrees in African American Studies. Panthers and their supporters regarded these organizing efforts as steps to implement point number of their platform.[42]

The 1970 Black Student Revolutionary Conference was another occasion of Panther-student cooperation. The conference was to build support for Bobby

Seale and the New Haven 14 (see chapter 3). Attendees heard speeches from Panther leaders and students who were active in party chapters throughout the country. Panel participants discussed such issues as cultural nationalism versus revolutionary nationalism, political prisoners, revolutionary art, and national salvation and self-defense.[43]

The Panthers usually succeeded in alliances and coalitions that operated on the basis of mutual respect. In other words, they had to extend the same respect to other organizations that they demanded for themselves. It took a certain political maturity to recognize that groups could unite around specific interests without dominating each other. This maturity, however, was only developed through experience, and it took several years before the BPP had the requisite background.[44]

The pressing need to recruit allies in the face of overwhelming government pressure encouraged the Panthers to organize a United Front against Fascism Conference in 1969. More than three thousand young white radicals, Latinos, Asians, Peace and Freedom Party members, black students, and members of other African American groups attended.[45]

Many of the attendees, however, did not necessarily agree with the party's categorization of the United States as a fascist entity. The ultimate implications of that assertion could entail a commitment to armed struggle. Many of the potential allies refused to take that fateful step. Many debates also arose over nonmembers submitting to Panther leadership even though the BPP considered itself the vanguard of the American front for international revolution.

Panther defense attorney Charles Garry summed up the general feeling of many white delegates by merely agreeing that political repression existed for some black and brown communities. This did not mean, however, that the entire country was in a state of fascism. The United Front against Fascism Conference did not build the grand alliance the Panthers had hoped for, but it did demonstrate that the BPP believed the struggle was between classes, not races. The party's pragmatic refusal to burn racial bridges also meant it could continue fund-raising in the white community.

The BPP continued its attempts to build alliances in 1970. It called for an interracial Revolutionary People's Constitutional Convention (RPCC). Eldridge Cleaver initiated the concept in 1968 to implement point number ten of the Panther platform. Point number ten called for a UN-supervised plebiscite to determine the national destiny of black people. Cleaver had waged a two-year campaign within the party for this meeting. He argued that the convention could be used to organize domestic and foreign support for the party. The BPP claimed to have polled several third-world UN delegates in 1968 and found them receptive to the idea of a plebiscite.[46]

In their public call for the convention, the Panthers maintained that a long train of abuses suffered by blacks had prompted the move and that other ethnic groups as well as white youth were victims of the ruling elite. The BPP believed a new constitution was necessary to implement a new political order that would ensure the people's liberties.

The Panthers also reminded the public that African Americans were armed and relied on military power to be the ultimate guarantor of their rights. The Panther Party claimed to speak for the majority of African Americans but offered no proof that other blacks believed in its argument.[47]

Matters became complicated, however, when Newton was released from jail after his conviction was overturned. The central committee discovered he opposed the RPCC idea.[48] Newton argued that the party had become too militaristic in his absence, and he believed the plan to create a national popular front through the convention ran counter to his vision for the Panthers.

Newton also claimed he wanted stronger local organizations working for the survival programs and an avoidance of further confrontations with the police.[49] He did not explain, however, how the RPCC would undermine either local control or survival programs. Nor did he explain how the party's current military stance differed from his own earlier advocacy of armed struggle.[50]

In reality Newton was wary of Cleaver's increasing influence. He had begun to view Cleaver as a rival for control of the party. Newton's stance placed him in the unique position of repudiating his earlier words and privately condemning Cleaver for implementing the Panthers' own call for a UN plebiscite in the ten-point program.

The RPCC was conceived of as a two-stage affair. An opening plenary session was scheduled for Philadelphia's Temple University over Labor Day. The plenary session was to be followed by another meeting scheduled for Washington, D.C., in November. The Philadelphia sessions got off to a rocky start because there was a spate of attacks on police the weekend preceding the convention. Even though the party was not involved in any of these incidents, the police attacked three Philadelphia Panther offices. The BPP believed the authorities were attempting to intimidate it into canceling the RPCC.[51]

The intimidation tactics failed, and an estimated ten thousand people attended the Philadelphia session. Newton's reluctance to become fully engaged in the RPCC, however, undermined the proceedings internally. In addition, despite months of propaganda, the Panthers had not done enough work to prepare adequately for the convention. They were simply overwhelmed by the logistics and preferred to emphasize Newton's speech rather than the workshops.

Still, convention workshops covered topics that ranged from self-determination for national minorities to control of the educational system to religious oppression.[52] Organizers claimed that the ideas drafted during the workshops were to be presented and accepted during the sessions in Washington, D.C. Nevertheless, a Panther leader admitted that the convention was mainly an educational affair to unite people behind the BPP because the party lacked any political power to implement proposed changes to the constitution.

Newton's reluctance to participate fully also helped to undermine the November 27–29 convention in Washington. A mainly white crowd, variously estimated at twenty-five hundred to five thousand people, arrived to find that a dispute over the rental fee had rendered Howard University's facilities unavailable. The Panthers claimed that Howard had reneged on a previous agreement to stage the convention, and the participants were left mainly to their own devices for two days. Newton said that the convention had been converted into a mobilization of the people for survival until after the revolution was completed.[53]

The *Black Panther* advised its readers that they should think about formulating a new constitution for the world that was in keeping with Newton's new political vision.[54] During his incarceration Newton had concluded that nation-states were outdated because capitalism ignored borders and governments while transforming the world into a network of oppressed and interdependent communities. Newton maintained that these communities should unite around a new philosophy that he called revolutionary intercommunalism.

Revolutionary intercommunalism would resist capitalism's reactionary intercommunalism. Newton's philosophy encountered resistance from a confused rank and file. They did not understand the logic behind the transition or the distinction between intercommunalism and the previous alliances with third-world countries.[55]

Some party supporters accused the Panthers of being ideologically inconsistent, and in fact they were correct. Newton, however, had another agenda that had nothing to do with consistency. He believed that he needed to distinguish himself from Cleaver and his continuous calls for armed struggle. Controlling the party's ideology was one tool to accomplish this end.

The International Struggle

The fourth aspect Malcolm influenced was the arena of international relations. The Free Huey movement carried the Panthers into the United Nations in 1968. They petitioned the General Assembly to station observer teams throughout the United States to protect blacks from an alleged genocidal war by the U.S. government.[56]

The Panthers claimed that Newton's murder trial was the first move in this plan, but they failed to convince enough member states to challenge the American government on a domestic matter. The major objective of the initiative was to obtain publicity for Newton's case. Panthers also believed the campaign implemented Malcolm's idea of building international alliances to assist blacks with their domestic agenda.

The BPP cultivated fraternal relations with third-world governments to carry out this idea. It also established an international section when Eldridge and Kathleen Cleaver went into exile (see chapter 3). Panthers thought their socialist orientation broadened the basis for their political contacts. In fact, they were able to have talks with the Vietnamese National Liberation Front. The NLF, however, was under no illusions about the Panthers' ability to defeat the U.S. government. It is more likely that the group was trying to build support for its own struggle by playing on U.S. internal divisions.

Huey Newton and Bobby Seale adapted Malcolm's ideas to fit the Panther Party. The BPP engaged in self-defense, organizing the underclass, interracial alliances, and international relations. Its organizing efforts were intense but had mixed results. Blacks and whites would support Newton during his trial because they believed the charges were a police frame-up.

Outrage at government misconduct or violence against blacks also united African Americans. In fact, a wave of urban rebellions swept the nation in the 1960s. The outbreaks were especially severe after Dr. Martin Luther King's assassination. Black militants did not know it at the time, but these uprisings were not the prelude to a revolution. They were, instead, temporary outbreaks of frustration and anger.

The long-range response of the black community would be more pragmatic. Politicians would be elected to represent aggrieved communities. Carl Stokes, a black Ohio legislator, became Cleveland's first African American mayor in 1970. Ron Dellums, a Berkeley city councilman, was elected to Congress in 1970 and eventually became chairman of the House Armed Services Committee. Coleman Young, a Michigan state senator from 1965 to 1973, became Detroit's first African American mayor in 1979. Other lesser-known blacks were also elected to office around the nation.

The majority of blacks believed they could succeed in America if racial prejudice was eliminated or restricted legally. They did not think their quest for justice and an end to prejudice was a mandate to attack the government.

As a result, the Panthers were beginning to be isolated as early as 1968. The BPP began to experiment with white allies to secure Newton's release from prison and bring additional resources to its organization. The party's alliance with whites facilitated a dramatic shift from Black Nationalism to socialism. The Panthers initially espoused Black Nationalism, but this philosophy proved to be too confining racially as well as politically amorphous.

Black Nationalist ideology was capable of containing the NOI's black capitalism and SNCC's third-world flirtations with communist Cuba and Nkrumah's Ghana. Furthermore, black Democrats and Republicans also claimed to be working for power and autonomy within mainstream political organizations.

Consequently, Black Nationalism threatened to isolate the BPP and increase the difficulty of freeing Newton. The Panthers recruited white allies to avoid this trap. The Panthers also became socialists because they believed it was a share-the-wealth philosophy that would transfer economic power to an oppressed black community. Furthermore, a socialist identity increased the domestic and international contacts that would assist in their battle for survival.

Nevertheless, even though the Panthers were allied with a number of organizations and individuals, the BPP insisted on defining the terms of the relationship. The Panther Party wanted to be certain it achieved the maximum benefit from any interracial alliance. Because the Panthers were usually in a precarious legal situation, the benefit was often some form of material or financial support. Ideological alliances on the international level were also designed to pub-

licize the Panther struggle against the American government in the hope of securing better treatment for the organization.

The Panther Party believed it was the heir to Malcolm, and the Muslim
minister did influence it in several important matters. The BPP ideology was
very flexible, though. The party's leaders were capable of changing to accom-
modate the prevailing political situation. Throughout the years the ten-point
program was the essence of their ideology, and it was this platform that attracted recruits from around the nation to the Panther cause.

2

SURVIVAL PENDING REVOLUTION

The Free Breakfast for School Children is about to cover the country and be initiated in every Chapter and Branch of the Black Panther Party....Our children need a nourishing breakfast every morning so they can learn.

—*Black Panther,* April 1969

The Black Panther Party occupied a precarious position from its inception. Patrolling the police and marching on Sacramento were bold initiatives. These actions attracted recruits to the organization and drew attention to the ten-point program and platform. These steps, however, severely circumscribed the party's future ideological and pragmatic choices because the government considered the BPP an armed threat to its authority.

Intense and unrelenting government pressure forced the party to go on the defensive. At the same time, enhanced economic opportunities and increased political and judicial representation threatened to isolate the Panthers by rechanneling dissent. It was the beginning of a classic carrot-and-stick operation.

It became obvious to some of the Panther leaders by 1969 that an armed revolution in the United States was not likely. The BPP discovered that as long as there were options, African Americans (like most of humanity) preferred political reform to the dangerous stresses of revolution. Revolutionary rhetoric had to be toned down if the Panthers were to survive. On the other hand, the government might allow survival programs to exist with no obviously dangerous consequences for the party. The choice may have been difficult, but it was also obvious.

Breakfast programs, liberation schools, and medical clinics became the preferred method of community organizing. These programs were not based on armed force. Instead, mass politicization, persuasion, and education were used to spread the Panther message. Community action enabled the BPP to survive disciplinary problems and government oppression. A much-needed breathing space was created for the central committee to reflect on the best method to ensure organizational survival.

For many members the survival programs defined their relationship with the party and the black community. New organizing methods attracted a different and more disciplined membership. Serving the people body and soul would become the watchword.

The struggle would be long and difficult, but the party would both seek and exploit the new opportunities that would be presented. The *Black Panther* succinctly stated the new political position: "Revolution cannot be carried out by words alone....The overthrow of one class by another must be carried out by revolutionary violence. Until this stage is achieved we must concentrate on the immediate needs of the people, in order to build a united political force, based on the ideology of the Black Panther Party. Survival pending Revolution is our immediate task and to do this we must meet the needs of the people...through our liberation schools, free breakfast programs, and child care centers."[1]

The Black Panther Party's survival programs, i.e., free breakfasts for schoolchildren, liberation schools, free medical clinics, and clothing programs, were some of the organization's best-known activities. Huey Newton maintained that the survival programs were designed to meet the material needs of African Americans while educating the community to a higher level of revolutionary consciousness:

> The original vision of the party was to develop a lifeline to the people, by serving their needs and defending them against their oppressors....We knew that this strategy would raise the consciousness of the people and give us their support....For a time the Black Panther Party lost its vision and defected from the community....The only reason the Party is still in existence at this time is because of the Ten Point Program...our survival program. Our programs would be meaningless and insignificant if they were not community programs.[2]

Contrary to Newton's assertions, however, the survival programs were not a part of the party's original activities in 1966; they did not appear until January 1969. The Panthers did not believe that the patrolling of police or the 1967 demonstration in Sacramento would qualify as survival programs because the skills were not readily transferable and could only be practiced at great personal risk. Newton admitted this during a 1971 essay in the party newspaper:

> When the Party went to Sacramento and...when the Party patrolled the police with arms, we were acting (in 1966) when the people had given up the philosophy of non-violent direct action and were beginning to deal with sterner stuff. We wanted them to see the virtues of disciplined and organized armed self-defense, rather than spontaneous and disorganized outbreaks and riots. Later...we discouraged actions like Sacramento and police observations because we recognized that these were not the things to do in every situation or on every occasion.[3]

The community programs obviously addressed real needs. Objectively, however, they were more important to the existence of the party as an organization than they were to the survival of the black community. Survival programs were originally instituted not only to serve the people but also to improve the party's image in the black community by providing positive, disciplined activities for the membership.

The Panther Party also envisioned the community programs as introducing socialism in practical and concrete terms. Donations solicited from businesses were a means of redistributing wealth from the haves to the have-nots.[4]

The party's community action programs also exemplified a basic tenet of Panther philosophy that was expressed by Huey Newton: "The Black Panther Party feels that the present government and its subsidiary institutions are illegitimate because they fail to relate to the people and they fail to meet the needs of the people. Therefore they have no right to exist....There is no excuse in our modern times for people to be without the basic necessities of life."[5]

Breakfast Programs

Landon Williams, central committee member, and Doug Miranda, a captain in the Boston BPP chapter, have credited Bobby Seale with initiating the community action concept and advocating its spread throughout the party's national structure.[6] A brief anecdote, supplied by Williams, explains how Seale happened on the idea.

The BPP had established an advisory committee during the 1968 Free Huey movement. The committee provided civilian input and broadened the Panther Party's political base in the black community. The committee complained to Seale in late 1968 that Panthers were drinking in public outside the party headquarters. Public drinking may have been a minor concern that could have been addressed internally, but there were other issues as well. These more serious issues threatened to tarnish the BPP's political image.

A few undisciplined Panthers, in a series of racially motivated incidents, attacked members of the hippie community. Other members had engaged in a series of robberies. These acts caused a great deal of embarrassment and highlighted the need for tighter discipline, political education, and a clearly defi mission for the members.[7]

Newton's manslaughter conviction in August 1968 had eliminated mass rallies as a major party activity. During the fall and winter of 1968 most Panther activities consisted of selling newspapers and "little red books," i.e., *Quotations from Chairman Mao.*

Seale met with party members to discuss resolving the disciplinary issue. Party member Wendell Wade commented that schoolchildren were passing his house every day, and they looked hungry. Wade jokingly suggested they should provide meals to schoolchildren as a method of furnishing positive activities for the membership. This suggestion led to a discussion about school performance and how hunger affected a child's ability to concentrate and learn. Seale responded by stating that even if the party could not "put a chicken in every basket, they could put a breakfast in every hungry kid's stomach."[8]

In January 1969 the central committee began an intensive drive to correct disciplinary and ideological problems within the BPP. Internal political education classes, tighter discipline, and community service received greater emphasis. New recruitment was halted, and in March 1969 thirty Oakland members were expelled for disciplinary infractions.[9]

In a March 1969 interview Seale also identified four new activities around which the party would be organizing: "The four key programs we are trying to implement are: the breakfast program, which is going on now; the petition campaign for the community control of police; free health clinics in the black community; and black liberation schools in the black community. Some people are going to call these programs reformist but we're revolutionaries.... It is one thing when the capitalists put it up and another thing when the revolutionary camp puts it up."[10]

Seale meant that the party would organize these survival programs to educate the community about the contradictions in a capitalist society between rich and poor. The Panthers wanted to point out that they were serving the needs of the people with limited resources while the government was doing nothing to alleviate the distress of hungry schoolchildren.

Seale ignored government initiatives such as the food stamp program. Nevertheless, his argument possessed a certain internal logic that was beneficial to the party. Seale could link the BPP's community service programs with political education, purges, and external attacks on the party by government agents:

> For the next three to six months we will be concentrating on raising the political consciousness within the party to a very high level. At the same time we will be going forth with our community programs....This program also helps more people relate to the party. They see that the party is not a bunch of avaricious fools. We have kicked out the people who robbed those banks and robbed those taverns and liquor stores for 200 and 300 and 80 dollars.... They will relate to the fact that the Party is really trying to serve them.[11]

Seale was correct in stating that the government wanted to destroy the party. The survival programs were intended to preserve the BPP's viability within the black and progressive communities. The BPP'S first free breakfast program for schoolchildren opened on January 20, 1969, at St. Augustine's Episcopal Church in Oakland, California. The party newspaper began advertising for program volunteers and equipment in the winter of 1968. The advertisements had first mentioned the Concord Baptist Church in Berkeley, but by December 1968 the site had been moved to St. Augustine's and the Black Community Center, both in Oakland.[12]

The community initiatives were first instituted in California. For example, the Vallejo, California, branch wrote an article for the Panther newspaper stating it had opened a free breakfast program for children. It was also soliciting donations. A second article also announced the expulsion of twenty-six individuals in order to guarantee the party's survival and to set correct examples for the people. The expelled members were characterized as reactionaries, but no further details of their activities were provided.[13]

The Vallejo chapter had obviously modeled its actions on the events that occurred in Oakland two months previously. Clearly this local branch had understood and demonstrated the nexus among community action programs, tighter discipline, and political survival. Breakfast programs also became mandatory for all branches throughout the country.

BPP members would encourage children to participate by distributing ers throughout communities and outside schools. Once some children began coming in the morning, the word would spread about the good and substantial meals. Other neighborhood children would quickly follow. Area businesspeople would be solicited by Panthers to supply food and utensils. Monetary donations were also requested.

The Panthers also used the programs to demonstrate the need for improved nutritional standards in the black community. The breakfast program's national coordinator claimed that twenty-two chapters and branches around the country had served twenty thousand children (or meals) by November 1969.[14]

This estimate is not unreasonable, considering that twenty-two offices offered the breakfast program. These figures would mean that approximately 688 children per office were fed each month. Many chapters were located in cities with large black populations (e.g., Chicago, New York, Los Angeles, Philadelphia, Baltimore, Kansas City, San Francisco, Oakland, Denver, Indianapolis, Milwaukee, Jersey City, New Haven, and Boston). In addition, many of these large cities had multiple sites that could easily have accommodated more than one hundred children at any one of them.

The FBI feared that the breakfast program would be used to teach children to hate police and spread antiwhite propaganda. Churches that allowed the Panthers to use their facilities received special government attention. Father Frank Curran in San Diego was one of the first supporters of the breakfast program in southern California. The FBI's records show that the bureau responded by contacting Curran's superiors.[15] Government agents claimed to be parishioners outraged by the priest's actions.

A month later Father Curran was transferred to New Mexico, and the FBI pronounced itself satisfied that the priest had been neutralized. The FBI also mailed anonymous letters to public officials and persons they thought capable of swaying public opinion against party efforts to initiate or maintain community action programs.[16]

Local police organizations interfered with the breakfast program in a more direct fashion. The party newspaper reported actions ranging from attacking support rallies in Des Moines to spoiling food during raids on offices in New York. Another tactic, utilized in Richmond, California, was the spreading of rumors. The Panthers were accused of endorsing riots or poisoning food used in the breakfast program. Encouraging ministers or organizations to deny facilities for use by the Panthers was another ploy used by local police.[17]

The free breakfasts continued despite these obstacles. In fact, they became the Panthers' most successful and popular community activity. Panthers believed the donations solicited from businesspeople were a means to implement the third point of the ten-point program and platform, that is, the call for an end to the robbery of the black community by the capitalist. Contributions were a method of "sharing" business profits with the community.

Liberation Schools

Liberation schools also began in 1969. They became crucial elements in the organizing drive. Liberation schools were a familiar concept in the black community because they had been an organizing tactic used by Southern civil rights groups. The Southern liberation schools had served as a central location for explaining the civil rights movement to community members. They had also been used as ad hoc education sites and as a recruiting device for demonstrations and voting rights drives.[18]

Party liberation schools resulted from the good relations that began with the free breakfasts. Panthers began to encourage children to return for other activities. The San Francisco liberation school served twenty-five children daily. The weekly curriculum was as follows: Monday, history day; Tuesday, culture day; Wednesday, field trips; Thursdays, revolutionary films; and Friday, current events. Songs and games were utilized to convey the Panther message. Children learned how to recite and explain the ten-point program and platform.[19]

In Staten Island, New York, children aged seven to twelve were instructed in the "roots and essence of a people's revolution."[20] One teaching device designed to appeal to children was a cartoon illustrating the ten-point program and platform. The teaching tool was utilized originally in the San Francisco liberation school.

The curriculum at most liberation schools consisted of basic academic skills and current events gleaned from newspapers and party literature. Community volunteers and Panthers staffed the schools. Some volunteers were college students who were able to impart a semblance of professional instruction at their locations.

Professional academic instruction, however, was not the primary goal of the liberation schools from 1969 to 1971. Instruction in Panther ideology and African American history were the most important items in the curriculum. This was not only because the Panthers lacked the expertise to do anything else but also because the academic potential of the liberation schools was not yet recognized by the leadership. That oversight was corrected within two years.

The Panther Party's most successful educational program was established in 1971 as the Intercommunal Institute. The name was changed to the Oakland Community School (OCS) in 1975. In 1973, the school moved to a multipurpose facility called the Oakland Community Learning Center under the nonprofit Educational Opportunities Corporation. The Community Learning Center also had a night school where adults studied for their general equivalency diplomas, or GEDs. There were sixteen accredited instructors and fifteen volunteers and aides. The school's director, Ericka Huggins, served on the Alameda County Board of Education.[21]

The OCS not only offered a quality private-school education but also instilled a sense of self-worth. OCS's day program offered a full curriculum to students aged two and one-half to eleven. Subjects covered language arts, Spanish, mathematics, science, social science, environmental studies, physical education, performing arts, and visual arts.

The school provided three full meals a day, referrals for preventive health care, and three passenger buses for transporting children to and from school. There was no tuition. Long-standing party rules had formerly prevented the Panthers from accepting government money.[22] This prohibition was quietly dropped in the early 1970s. The OCS became eligible to apply for and accept state education funds. Private foundation grants, state education grants, and community fund-raising helped to support the school. The actual cost per child was approximately $720 per year. The cost of operating the OCS was

$6,000 per month, and the budget for the Community Learning Center was $100,000 per year.[23]

At the height of its enrollment, the school served four hundred students from all ethnic backgrounds. It once received an award from Governor Jerry Brown and the California legislature for "having set the highest level of elementary education in the state."[24] The state Department of Education also cited OCS as offering one of the most important models for elementary children in the inner city, demonstrating that quality education for inner-city children could be achieved despite substantial social obstacles.

The school, in fact, lived longer than the BPP. The Panthers ceased functioning in 1980; the OCS survived as an independent entity and graduated its last class in 1982. It was the last remnant of the Panther Party.

Medical Clinics

The Panthers believed that the urban health care system for blacks mirrored the institutional racism of American society. Historically, most black doctors had been educated at either Fisk or Howard universities. White southern medical colleges traditionally admitted no black students, and northern medical schools educated only a few.[25]

Panthers began working with sympathetic members of the medical community in 1969 to provide services and information primarily in preventive health care. The BPP established free medical clinics in Kansas City, Seattle, Los Angeles, Berkeley, New Haven, Portland, Chicago, Rockford (Illinois), Boston, Philadelphia, and multiple sites in New York.[26]

The BPP Staten Island health cadre recruited "revolutionary doctors" who provided house calls to needy community people.[27] They treated anemia, worms, malnutrition, weapon injuries, hearing and vision, and gum diseases. The Staten Island office also gave free physical exams and draft counseling to young men.

The party health cadre was responsible for providing the primary care for their comrades as well as distributing basic medical information to the community. Volunteer doctors and nurses trained party members. Panthers initially concentrated on acquiring basic first-aid skills, which they applied to their own colleagues in local chapters and branches. In the New York metropolitan area, the medical cadre from the Bronx, Brooklyn, Harlem, and Jamaica, Queens, met on a weekly basis to sustain joint activities and share medical technology.[28]

Two of the most successful medical programs operated in Chicago and Boston. The Spurgeon "Jake" Winters Clinic in Chicago was named after a Panther killed by police in November 1969. Panthers worked with medical professionals who provided expertise in the areas of gynecology, obstetrics, pediatrics, optometry, and dentistry. Volunteers and medical students canvassed the community to facilitate the provision of services and information. The BPP claimed the clinic served more than two thousand people during the first two months of its existence.[29]

The Boston People's Free Health Clinic opened in May 1970 in response to the police shooting death of a black patient at Boston General Hospital. The clinic provided similar services as the Chicago program, and in addition it trained lab technicians, nurse assistants, and medical secretaries.[30]

In 1971 the Black Panther Party launched a national testing program for sickle cell anemia and worked to establish a research foundation for ending the disease. Dr. Tolbert Small (based in Berkeley, California) was the national chairman of the Panther Party's Sickle Cell Anemia Project. The BPP's free clinics tested and counseled more than one million black patients about sickle cell anemia. Panthers believed that President Richard Nixon began a government sickle cell program to counter the political appeal of the Panther initiative.

The Panther Party contended that American health care was a tool to "strengthen the ruling class" and argued that medicine's goal should be the well-being of the people, not profit.[32] Panthers accused the health industry of facilitating a doctor shortage (monopoly) so high fees could be charged, maintaining high prices for drugs, and underpaying nurses' aides and janitors. The BPP believed it would be setting an example of socialism and self-determination by instituting a free program.

The Panthers believed that socialism was a share-the-wealth philosophy that should concentrate on distribution. The BPP ignored any economic aspects related to production. Panthers maintained that free services at their clinics had solved the problem of medical professionals alienating themselves from the very people they claimed to be serving.[33]

Preventive health care was also manifested in sporadic attempts to combat the drug epidemic, which infested many black communities. Michael "Ceta-wayo" Tabor, a New York Panther, had been a drug addict prior to joining the party. He was arrested in 1969 with other Panthers and charged with conspiring to bomb public facilities. The group was acquitted in 1971 after a lengthy trial.

Tabor wrote a pamphlet while he was incarcerated that defined the drug epidemic as another example of the black community's political oppression. Tabor called for another approach to solving drug addiction that would substitute community development and self-determination as positive regenerative activities for self-defeating addiction.[34] This concept was another manifestation of the Malcolm X–inspired belief that personal involvement in struggle was capable of morally reclaiming America's dispossessed.

The BPP medical program had a long-lasting effect on the community because party members learned valuable technical skills they would be able to practice years after they left the Panthers. For some, however, there were negative consequences to political involvement. For example, the FBI unsuccessfully attempted to have Dr. Small fired from his job at Oakland's Highland Hospital by informing the administration that he worked with the Black Panther Party. The FBI also arranged for the shah of Iran's secret police, SAVAK, to detain an Iranian medical technician who had volunteered to work in Berkeley's George Jackson Free Clinic.[35]

Not all survival programs achieved the same level of success. The national petition drive for community control (decentralization) of police was more sporadic in nature and was not thoroughly publicized until August 1969 when it was highlighted in the party newspaper. Panthers attempted to organize electoral opposition to police brutality by initiating a referendum process that would establish separate police departments in cities with large black populations.

The BPP claimed the campaign was a fundamental challenge to the government because it threatened an important arm of state power. The Panthers knew full well that the initiative process had little probability of success. Nevertheless, they were willing to utilize the electoral process as an organizing tool for the transmission of their political message. Petitions were circulated in each chapter, but the main focus remained on clinics, schools, and breakfast programs.[36]

Political Education

Mandatory attendance in political education (PE) classes was an essential part of the BPP's rectification campaign. Political education classes started in 1966 when Seale and Newton began reading Malcolm X, Frantz Fanon, and Mao Zedong. Political education for the general membership continued on a sporadic basis throughout 1967 and 1968. Classes were organized for members to read the *Quotations from Chairman Mao* and Huey Newton's *Essays from the Minister of Defense.*

The party newspaper also published a BPP book list, which included works from Herbert Aptheker, Basil Davidson, John Hope Franklin, William Patterson, J. A. Rogers, and C. Vann Woodward. It was unclear, however, whether the list was recommended for party members or for the general public who wanted to improve their knowledge of African and African American history.[37] There were, however, a few Panthers who studied some of the books on the list.

The experience that Billy X. Jennings had with PE was typical of many members who joined in 1968. Jennings was encouraged to join after visiting an office in East Oakland. He became a Panther-in-training for six weeks. During that time he had to conduct himself as a regular member and demonstrate an understanding of the party's philosophy and history. Jennings recalled that "Wendell Wade and Landon Williams taught political education at that time, and he remembered being told that he should study at least two hours a day from readings on the book list.[38]

Political education on a more formal basis began in 1969 when Bobby Seale announced mandatory classes for members throughout the nation in order to improve their understanding of BPP history and revolutionary theory.[39] classes were conducted weekly, and members usually read assigned selections from the BPP newspaper and *Quotations from Chairman Mao* that focused on discipline, revolutionary aphorisms, and the evils of capitalism.

This pocket-sized text was, as noted earlier, commonly known as the "little red book." In 1969 party members usually carried the red book in their back pocket and were ready to pull it out at a moment's notice to prove some ideological point.

Newspaper material focused on editorials or particular campaigns in which the party was engaged, such as circulating petitions for community control of police. Members would discuss the week's readings, and a group leader would answer questions.

Assata Shakur, a New York Panther, remembered that most of her PE classes consisted of memorizing and reciting slogans from the red book without truly understanding their meaning or context. This practice tended to frustrate those Panthers who were more advanced educationally.[40]

Shakur recalled a troubling incident about political education: an African supporter had donated a calendar with pictures of guerilla fighters urging international support of African liberation. A party official discarded the calendar in 1971 when the BPP changed its philosophy to intercommunalism. The official believed that it was incorrect to keep the calendar because internationalism could now be considered "wrong."[41]

Shakur maintained that PE classes instilled a rudimentary level of knowledge about BPP affairs and basic Marxism. There were, however, no required readings by African American scholars or on African American history. This material could have put the PE classes in a more familiar context.

Outside reading to enhance one's understanding of African American history or political affairs was often criticized as petit bourgeois or cultural nationalist. Shakur remembered there were some Panthers reading Mao but for the most part "didn't know who Harriet Tubman, Marcus Garvey, and Nat Turner were."[42]

Still, the problem was more complex than the curriculum. The Panther program also fell short of its goal because many members had received an inferior public school education. Public schools had not prepared most of them for critical study. Bobby Seale recognized this reality in 1973 when he acknowledged that "many people in the collective" needed remedial reading and math. Seale recommended dividing PE classes into two groups, an advanced and a secondary group, because a "large portion of the comrades in the secondary group did not finish high school."[43]

Community PE classes were held for the purpose of teaching the general public about the ten-point program, survival programs, and different current events that appeared in the BPP newspaper or the mainstream press. Rank-and-file members were encouraged to write editorials or articles for the BPP newspaper that articulated organization history and ideology.

Panthers took the opportunity to write articles that traced the history of black rebellion and condemned American foreign policy, capitalism, and cultural nationalism. African Americans were exhorted to accept the BPP's leadership, and whites were called on to organize in their own communities. These positive activities allowed rank-and-file members to have a sense of ownership about party policy, which was invaluable in building morale and a sense of purpose.[44]

Panther leaders had their own PE classes. A BPP ideological institute was organized in 1970 to advance the study of Marxism and to improve the BPP internal functioning.[45] Party leaders taught the rank and file that a small body within the central committee, called the political bureau, would make all difficult decisions. The political bureau formally consisted of Newton, Seale, and David Hilliard.

All decisions made by this part of the central committee were binding on the rank and file without any dissent, although explanations (i.e., "discussion were allowed. This method was called democratic centralism and led to complaints from the rank and file that the governing style was "all centralism and no democracy."[46] These grievances would come back to haunt the party in later years when accusations of fraud were accompanied by charges that the BPP leadership lacked transparency and accountability.

Evaluating the Survival Programs

The survival programs began because the BPP needed a new organizational focus in order to survive as a relevant political entity in the black community. The new focus had to be capable of engaging members in productive and disciplined activities while serving as a model for community development and education for the party's constituency. Just as important, any changes had to conform to an ideological model that would be accepted by the membership.

Socialism as a revolutionary share-the-wealth philosophy was the ideological model that could be accepted by the membership. Consequently, the survival programs were a pragmatic as well as an ideological response to real needs. The central committee had discovered through trial and error that patrolling the police as a principal means of organizing was unrealistic. Newton's incarceration, the lack of discipline and political education among some members, and government attacks forced the BPP to reevaluate its goals and methods.

This reevaluation resulted in the birth of the community action programs.

"Survival pending revolution" was a practical political move. Seale and other Panther leaders were convinced that a lifeline to the people must be built to enhance the party's chances for survival. Institutional survival was a necessary first step.

Institutional survival was the only opportunity to advocate the political message of self-determination and to continue the campaign to free Newton and the large numbers of other incarcerated Panthers. Reform programs were the most rational means to accomplish this objective.

The community action programs were intended to organize an effective opposition to the government's hostility to the Panther Party, recruit members, and facilitate public reception for the party's political message. Bobby Seale claimed that the most effective strategy to accomplish this goal was to provide needed goods and services while educating the community to its revolutionary potential. The ultimate purpose of community action was to ensure the party's survival through a broad base of community support.

The survival programs' effectiveness in addressing party and community needs may be assessed in several ways: the response of the community, the response of the party, and the response of the government to Panther organizing efforts. Community support for the survival programs can be determined from the number of people who received services, contributed time or money, and expressed verbal support for the maintenance of these programs.

As noted earlier, the BPP claimed to have served more than twenty thousand children by November 1969. The number of people who received medical services cannot be ascertained with any degree of finality. Still, it is certain that enough professionals participated in the medical clinics to enable the Panther Party to offer services in eleven cities.[47]

Political support can also be judged from other organizations initiating their own community programs. For example, Chicago Panthers worked with the Black Disciples street gang to begin a breakfast program.[48] Finally, survival programs can be evaluated to determine how they politically educated members and improved discipline by curtailing antisocial activities.

The rectification program created the space necessary for the Panthers to begin to expand their community action tactics. Undisciplined members were expelled, conduct began to be strictly regulated, and regular PE classes were instituted. These changes provided a disciplined and politically educated cadre who personified the BPP political message. Without this positive image the survival programs would have died for lack of participation by the community.

The community's participation in the programs validated Seale's initiative and foresight. In addition, essays in the *Black Panther* reflected the pride of the rank and file in "serving the people" because the survival programs were their creation. Party members wrote that they were demonstrating socialism to the black community by distributing obviously available goods and services to meet the needs of the people.

Panthers maintained that unequal distribution existed because of capitalism. Diahhne Jenkins argued this point by stating the following:

> The Black Panther Party is bringing the idea of socialism from a lower level to a higher level, with the initiation of the Liberation Schools, Free Breakfast Program, Free Lunch Program, Free Health Clinics, etc. These are all practices in socialism . . . so it is the responsibility of the Black Panther Party and every revolutionary to see to it that our people aren't neglected any longer. So the Black Panther Party will continue to develop these programs . . . and constantly raise the political level of the masses to the point where we, on a collective basis, will be organized and armed.[49]

Cheryl Simmons, like other members, joined the BPP because "the Panthers were doing something, they were feeding people, they were talking about taking care of the seniors in the community. In some cases they were providing childcare. Free medical centers were in the making. These were significant accomplishments and I thought I'd just check these people out."[50] Like other Panthers, Simmons believed that by redistributing goods and services, party members were providing a viable political alternative to capitalism.

This popular approach attracted supporters and allowed the BPP an opportunity to disseminate other aspects of their political platform and program. Bobby Seale contended that the breakfast program was socialistic because

> this weakens the power structure because the businessmen in the black community are the ones who have to donate to this program. . . . The first businessman who says he ain't gonna donate we're gonna tell the people in the community "Don't buy from him." Why? Because he won't donate one penny of every dollar for some breakfast. . . . We're educating the people through a practical functioning operation of a socialistic program. Once the

people see a socialistic program is valuable to them they won't throw it away. By practicing socialism they learn it better.[51]

The concept of production, however, was absent from this argument. All economic systems must address production as well as distribution. It was not enough merely to redistribute goods to the community under the banner of socialism because a capitalist government can and will accomplish the same task through social service agencies.

For an economic activity to be socialist, the party and the people must also be involved in production. This argument was never made at the time because the party did not intend the survival programs to be a business. Many community activists advocated socialism in the 1960s. The political and social systems of China, Cuba, Vietnam, Algeria, Guinea, and Tanzania were their ideological beacons.

Activists argued that capitalism had victimized African Americans in the slave trade and later through semiserfdom in the post–Civil War South. Furthermore, the practice of last hired and first fired was a frequent experience of blacks. Consequently, it is no surprise that capitalism was an anathema to Black Power advocates. Their personal and community experiences with capitalism had for the most part been negative ones.

But it was not necessary to become a capitalist to operate the community programs in a businesslike manner. For example, an alternative economic model already existed in Berkeley, where the cooperative grocery stores were owned by their membership. Many working and middle-class families joined by purchasing one or more shares for a six-dollar fee.

A board of directors oversaw daily operation of the facilities, provided professional managing expertise, and paid any dividends after operating expenses were deducted. This cooperative model successfully operated within a capitalist economy for many years. It provided a consumer-based alternative to large grocery chains.

Medical clinics owned by the BPP and doctors also might have proved their economic worth for alternative service delivery in the black community. Sympathetic medical volunteers had already demonstrated that they were available to provide services. Payment of monthly premiums for family health care could have created a sense of ownership and pride in the people served by the Panthers. The premiums could have operated on a sliding scale congruent with family income. Medicare patients would probably have been the bulk of the clientele, but both income streams may have been enough to achieve economic success.

At any rate, economic competition was not the only rationale for this model. The party's politics practically dictated the construction of a socially conscious model capable of demonstrating the financial feasibility of cooperative medical clinics. In a similar fashion the breakfast programs and the liberation schools might have been nonprofit operations with paid staff. All donations necessary for their maintenance could have been tax free.

The Oakland Community School did operate as a nonprofit institute, but the same benefit could have been extended much earlier to all party-operated liberation schools across the country. Jimmy Slater, a Cleveland Panther, phrased it in the following manner:

> I still don't think capitalism works, [but] you need capital to function in a capitalistic system. Upon reflection, this was one of the areas that I thought we were too liberal about during the black movement of the sixties. We wanted to give everything away and we were simply too liberal in our view. We know now that was an error. We had certain things the Black Panther Party had built and established; however, because of our hate for capitalism, *we didn't sustain anything* [emphasis added]. We had buildings and homes. We owned property. *We should have learned how to control the economy and to manage those things* [emphasis added]. Instead we wanted to fight against capitalism, and now we know that we should have established an economic base. In order to keep the movement going you've got to have capital.[52]

Slater confirms a critique of the survival programs for not transitioning to production and ownership. Despite its advocacy of socialism, the central committee missed the importance of establishing an economic base (especially in a capitalist society).

Production and distribution are two sides of the same coin in socialism. These arguments were not made at the time for a variety of reasons. The most pressing business was the survival of the party by creating a more disciplined membership and broadening the political base. All other considerations were secondary.

Nevertheless, after examining the historical record of the Panther Party survival programs, an argument can be made that alternative models may have increased their effectiveness. The argument is not what the Panthers should have known in 1969–71. They were under too much pressure for such a leisurely theoretical discussion. They did what they thought was best at the time.

From 1971 forward, however, as the programs became the primary basis for the existence of the party, an improvement in their organization was possible and desirable. The human cost of the party's political activities was very high, and out of respect for that sacrifice the BPP leadership should have considered a more scientific approach to their survival programs.

It is undeniably true that the government undermined the BPP's survival programs. It is equally true that the programs failed to reach their full potential because the distribution of goods and services was not sufficient to support either a reformist or a revolutionary position. The programs were vulnerable when the government (with greater resources) intensified its own outreach efforts.

There were economic and theoretical deficiencies in the survival programs that could have been corrected with relatively little difficulty. Once corrected, the programs could have served as a model of progressive community organizing for the entire country.

The BPP said that twenty-seven Panthers died from 1968 through 1973. Twenty-six lost their lives in violent confrontations, and one died in an automobile accident. Many others were incarcerated or endured severe hardships to implement the ten-point program and platform. The survival programs are an important part of Panther history. Improvements in the community programs would only have added to the rank-and-file's legacy.[53]

3

REGIONAL DEVELOPMENT OF THE BLACK PANTHER PARTY

The Black Panther Party supports you and all your efforts in your effort for the liberation of all black people.... Not only do we have 26 chapters of the Black Panther Party... but our struggle for liberation is supported by black, brown, red, and yellow brothers and sisters all over the world. Our Minister of Education, George Murray and Captain Ford of New York went to Cuba and the brothers and sisters there say The sky is the limit if our Minister of Defense, Huey P. Newton, is not set free.

—*Black Panther,* September 1968

From 1966 to 1971 the BPP grew from a small Oakland-based group to an international organization that operated at one time or another in sixty-one American cities and had more than two thousand members.[1] The Panther Party's rapid growth was fueled by its militant reputation, which attracted large numbers of adventurous and politically curious youth. Young blacks across the country became involved in the Free Huey campaign. Panther offices opened seemingly overnight, and urban streets were filled with demonstrators demanding not only Newton's freedom but also self-determination, community control of police, and an end to the Vietnam War.

The dangers of unregulated growth, however, quickly became clear when police infiltrators convinced some young Panthers to engage in provocative actions that resulted in many arrests and convictions. Others needed no persuading. They were convinced that the revolution had come and that it was time to pick up the gun.

By late 1968, however, the police were prepared to handle the earlier Panther tactics. These methods had become too dangerous and counterproductive. National headquarters discouraged conducting citizens' arrests, patrolling the police, and carrying weapons. Newton's conviction and the need for a more disciplined organization forced the central committee to begin purging undisciplined members and instituting PE classes and survival programs. The central committee tried to build a disciplined organization that would obey orders without asking questions.[2]

Community activists working in the Free Huey movement outside of California began claiming Panther status in 1968. Official charters, however, were only awarded to groups that agreed to meet the standards set by central headquarters in Oakland. Aspirants who wanted to begin chapters were summoned to Oakland (or came on their own) for six weeks of training, PE, and indoctrination in the ten-point program and platform and the party rules and regulations.

Volunteers also attended classes to learn administrative procedures. Local chapters were ordered to submit weekly written reports that covered organizing activities, progress in implementing programs, significant proposals for new operations, relations with other groups, and content of PE classes. Financial reports were to be filed monthly.[3]

Leaders were then approved to form a chapter and allowed to assume a title such as deputy chairman, deputy minister of defense, or defense captain. Local offices were controlled and vetted in this manner because the central committee wanted to exclude police agents and "rally Panthers." "Rally Panthers" were those who never worked on more mundane tasks. They specialized in showing up for special events where they could display their leather jackets and berets.[4]

The central committee also became familiar with out-of-state personnel through other means. A national retreat was held in November 1968, and an ideological institute for leaders was begun in 1970. These activities allowed members to become familiar with each other and party policy. Panthers believed these face-to-face relationships were very important in building trust and unity within their besieged organization.

There were thirteen BPP chapters, twenty National Committee to Combat Fascism (NCCF) offices, several community information centers, and an international section in Algiers. The NCCFs began in 1969 as a Panther organizing bureau after undisciplined elements were purged.[5] NCCFs sold the *Black Panther,* established community programs, held PE classes, subjected themselves to the same discipline, and adhered to the party's political line like regular chapters.

An NCCF office was sometimes started from a former Panther branch that had been disbanded for not having enough members or failing to obey orders. The NCCFs were technically open to whites. So far as is known, however, whites worked only in the Berkeley, California, office. Black NCCF offices saw membership as an opportunity to demonstrate their suitability for full BPP chapter status. For instance, NCCF workers opened offices in Winston-Salem in 1969 and in New Orleans in 1970, and the North Carolina group became a BPP chapter in 1971.

The NCCF branches also fit into the central committee's plan to move the party from a mass organization to a smaller, trusted membership of mostly full-time workers. Community information centers were another outreach effort. Their primary task was to supervise community programs and encourage non-Panthers to work with BPP survival programs. Community workers were not Panthers, but as part of their duties they were expected to be familiar with party ideology and history.[6]

The central committee periodically appointed such officials as June Hilliard, assistant chief of staff, Ray "Masai" Hewitt, minister of education, or Don Cox, field marshal, to supervise new branches. For the most part, however, manpower shortages at central headquarters usually prevented these inspection tours, and officials from nearby large chapters supervised smaller offices in their regions. For instance, the Chicago chapter exercised authority over Michigan and Indiana. The New York office occasionally supervised the Philadelphia Panthers, and Kansas City supervised the Des Moines and Omaha offices when ordered to do so by central headquarters.[7]

Discipline was maintained by ordering errant local officials to national headquarters or by having a regional official investigate and report to the national office. Disciplinary action included verbal warnings, suspensions, and expulsions. In extreme cases entire chapters could be closed. The Detroit branch was disbanded in the summer of 1969 after the deputy minister of defense was fatally shot in the party office and no explanation was given to central headquarters. An NCCF was organized to handle subsequent affairs in Detroit.

The Omaha branch was expelled in 1969 for accepting government funds in violation of BPP rules, and a later NCCF was also disbanded for other infractions. The Des Moines branch was terminated in March 1970 for nonperformance of duties after the office was bombed. The Kansas City, Missouri, of was shut down in 1970 after its leader, Pete O'Neal, went into exile following weapons charges and the chapter had dwindled to eight members.[9]

Local chapters often had difficulty remaining financially solvent. They relied on sales of the party newspaper, speakers' fees, and donations from organizations and individuals for financial support. The *Black Panther* was not only the voice of the party but an important income resource as well. National headquarters imposed quotas for newspaper sales based on the size of the chapter and required payment for the previous week before a new shipment was sent. The paper sold for twenty-five cents a copy, and twelve and one-half cents was remitted to central headquarters. Central headquarters realized five cents profit after deductions for production and distribution costs. The local chapter often gave five cents to the sellers as an incentive and kept seven and one-half cents to defray expenses.[10]

Newspaper sales reflected the party's political appeal and the organizational ability of the local branches. Circulation figures were high when the branches had an active membership enthused about spreading the party's message. The FBI estimated that the *Black Panther* had a worldwide weekly circulation exceeding 139,000 in 1970. That figure was slashed to fifty thousand in 1972 after the BPP's appeal began to falter. The BPP struggled in 1979 to raise four hundred dollars to print a biweekly newspaper with a circulation of only fifty-five hundred in Oakland, Chicago, Detroit, and Milwaukee.[11] The newspaper's last year of publication was 1980.

Expenses for local chapters included communal shelter, meals for full-time Panthers, travel funds (gas for cars and out-of-town travel), printing, office rent, and bail money and other legal expenses. Merchants in the black community were aggressively lobbied for food and donations to the community programs. Some of these supplies were allocated for the use of members.[12]

Donations and contributions from white allies such as churches, students, and political sympathizers helped to support many local chapters and national causes in 1970. A congressional investigation revealed that a New York donor contributed $20,000 for Huey Newton's bail. Another supporter donated $17,000, and an additional $10,000 was raised at a cocktail party sponsored by music conductor Leonard Bernstein. The Methodist Inner City Parish in Kansas City provided Panthers with employment, rent-free offices, bail money, and a van for food distribution. White sympathizers assisted the BPP in Ann Arbor, Des Moines, and Indianapolis with cash and credit cards.[13]

Panthers also raised funds by selling posters, buttons, badges, and literature. The speech-making circuit was especially lucrative in 1968, the year Bobby Seale received from $500 to $1,000 for appearances. Panthers made

189 speeches in 1969, and some fees were as high as $1,900. Huey Newton requested $2,500 for a speech in 1970.[14]

These income sources were not the norm for ordinary members, however. Party leaders preferred that the rank and file become full-time Panthers to ensure loyalty and efficiency. This meant ordinary members often had a subsistent living standard because their income came from limited sources, such as paper sales or student financial aid.[15]

This practice continued until it became too great a hardship for the small cadre of surviving members. Many Panthers were working by 1977, and some were collecting welfare as well. Collecting welfare was not limited to the rank and file, however; in 1977 the Alameda County welfare department in Oakland sued Ericka Huggins (head of the BPP Community School) to collect overpayments.[16]

As noted earlier, chapters and branches were originally prohibited by party rules from accepting grants, poverty funds, or aid from any government agency without contacting central headquarters. This amounted to a ban on receiving government funds because party leadership did not want any governmental control or oversight.[17] This prohibition was observed until 1971. At that time the BPP Educational Opportunities Corporation began receiving antipoverty funds for payroll and operating expenses for the Oakland Community School system.

The BPP attempted to alleviate the financial burden on the rank and in 1979 after an internal audit found previous bookkeeping to be inconsistent. Cash allotments for living expenses were maligned as "unjust and sloppy. The audit also recommended that financial matters no longer remain secret to the rank and file. In fact, stipends and clothing accounts were to be issued to all members on the basis of need and regardless of rank. The Panther Party, however, had only one more year of existence, and small changes that would have made a great deal of difference to the membership in 1969 were too little and too late.

Southern Chapters

The formal standard for membership was a six-week probationary period. During this time a Panther in training was required to attend PE classes, sell the newspaper, work in survival programs, and memorize the ten-point program and platform.

Some chapters also required potential recruits to complete applications and submit to a background check, but this practice was rare. Most recruits simply walked into an office and volunteered for duty. Panthers became known as good or bad recruits through their actual work.[19]

Carl Hampton, the future leader of the Houston branch, was a traveling musician in 1969 when he began volunteering at the national office in Berkeley. The BPP was not accepting new members at the time, and he was unable to join.[20] Hampton, however, was not discouraged. He attended PE classes and sold papers before returning to Houston to found an organization called People's Party II (PPII). PPII was not officially affiliated with the BPP, but the group followed the party's political line, sold the *Black Panther,* and began organizing to rid the Houston ghetto of its notorious vice elements.[21]

Hampton's fervent manner soon attracted attention from the authorities. He had a confrontation with police when he came to the aid of a member who was selling papers without a permit. A warrant was issued for Hampton's arrest after the incident, and armed PPII members began guarding their headquarters. PPII members staged a rally on July 26, 1970, to publicize the issues.

The area around the headquarters was declared a secure zone that would be kept free of police. A black bail bondsman convinced Hampton that he was working on a surrender deal with the police and urged PPII members to go home. In the meantime a police sniper post was set up across the street from the PPII office. Hampton was lured into the open to investigate a report of armed white men in the neighborhood, and a police sniper killed him. A night of rioting followed his death.[22]

A community coalition emerged and began a brief unity movement among local black groups. The coalition charged police with killing twenty blacks accused of robbery in the preceding seven months. The coalition also demanded the firing of the police chief, the establishment of a civilian review board, an immediate review of police hiring procedures, and a review of conditions in city jails. With the exception of two officers indicted for stomping a suspect to death, no one was charged in any of the killings.[23]

PPII became a Panther office after Hampton's death. The chapter offered community programs such as a petition for community control of police and voter registration. In 1974 the chapter began training black students at Texas Southern University as screeners for sickle cell, hypertension, and diabetes. Party offices nationwide began to close down during the late 1970s, and the Houston office also shut its doors.[24]

Other Southern offices had a similar fate. Larry Little founded the Winston-Salem, North Carolina, NCCF office in the summer of 1969. The chapter ranged between fifteen and twenty members and approximately fifty supporters who functioned on a part-time basis when it achieved BPP chapter status in 1971. The office began free breakfasts for schoolchildren, a liberation school, a free clothing program, and a free ambulance service that functioned until 1976.

Circulation for the *Black Panther* in North Carolina reached a peak of three thousand in 1972. The office also incurred the active enmity of the local police and the Charlotte FBI office. Government documents released in 1976 revealed that the counterintelligence program wiretapped the office and circulated anonymous letters to BPP supporters alleging that children who attended the breakfast program were forced to commit homosexual acts before they were fed. The Panthers were also falsely accused of stealing money from their survival programs.[25]

The community was stunned by the charges because it had enthusiastically supported the party's programs. Some supporters suspected foul play but were unable to prove it. Others believed the letters originated with disgruntled black churchgoers who were afraid to speak out openly. More FBI letters falsely accused the Panthers of preparing for a shootout with the local police.

The FBI believed the weapons allegations would give the police an opportunity to implicate the Panthers if any confrontations occurred. The police arrest of four Panthers accused of stealing a meat truck provoked a shootout in January 1971. Little maintained that an unknown black man (presumably a police agent) had approached him and said that a meat company wanted to donate to the breakfast program. The Panthers accepted the offer, but after the truck's arrival a white man came with the police and accused them of theft. At this point the unknown black pulled a gun, and shots were allegedly fired from the party office. Police returned fire. The Panthers were arrested and charged with stealing the meat. Party lawyers were successful in having the charges dismissed after they raised questions about blacks being excluded from jury service.

Also, the Panther office caught fire in November 1970, and firefighters removed records from the building. The files contained lists of supporters. Months went by before they were returned. Little served a thirty-day sentence in 1970. The FBI tried to recruit him as an informer while he was incarcerated, but he refused. The Winston-Salem office remained loyal to Newton during the schism, and some members worked on Seale's election campaign. By 1978, however, they were no longer selling papers, and the office was closed.[26]

The New Orleans NCCF began in 1969 and was originally located adjacent to the city's Desire housing project. After a year of organizing, members and community volunteers were serving more than one hundred children daily at a combined breakfast program and liberation school. Public meetings supporting the party often drew up to 150 participants. Unfortunately for the Panthers, two of the participants in public meetings were undercover agents from the New Orleans police department. The agents had gained the trust of the local office before they were discovered in September 1970.[27]

The NCCF convened a "people's court," where the agents were accused and then beaten by Panthers and community members. The agents managed to escape and contacted other police officers.[28] Police attacked the office after claiming the occupants fired on them. Seven people were shot before sixteen NCCF members surrendered. Police were accused of beating the prisoners before taking them to jail. In response, community residents attempted to burn several stores later that night. Police killed an unarmed black civilian during the disturbances.[29]

Residents then took the unusual step of setting up an independent commission to establish the facts surrounding the deadly incident. The commission invited the mayor, police superintendent, district attorney, and U.S. attorney to testify. The police superintendent and the assistant district attorney appeared but declined to give any statements because of pending litigation against the NCCF.[30]

The NCCF moved its office into the Desire housing project in October and stayed there until the police evicted the group later in the year. The tumult in Louisiana continued in early 1971 when several BPP members fleeing murder charges in New York were captured in New Orleans. The national manhunt for the New York fugitives, combined with intense local police pressure, virtually destroyed the effectiveness of the New Orleans NCCF. The Louisiana chapter's effectiveness ended by 1972. The office went out of existence shortly thereafter.[31]

On the surface the incident at the Desire housing project resembled many other confrontations between police and Panthers. There were, however, differences. The beating of the two agents is strikingly similar to a 1969 New Haven incident that resulted in the death of a Panther. The incident also confirms David Hilliard's and Elaine Brown's statements on the use of physical discipline in the BPP (see chapter 4).

The "people's court" proceeding was not unusual. One of the problems, however, is the lack of thought that went into the whole procedure. It should have been clear that the New Orleans police were not going to allow two of their officers to be beaten or murdered with impunity. The New Haven and New Orleans incidents demonstrate that the Panthers believed they were at war. This belief justified taking extreme measures against their enemies.

It is just as obvious that the long-range consequences of "people's courts" were ignored. These extralegal procedures were dangerous because nothing positive could ever have been accomplished with them. The police were obviously not going to sacrifice their undercover agents. Scarce resources were deployed defending members against charges that could have easily been avoided. The names and pictures of presumed spies and malefactors could have simply been printed in the *Black Panther*. In fact, this was done several times. This single procedure would have prevented court battles and avoided damaging the party's reputation in the community.[32]

The alternative "courts" never worked. In any case, the NCCFs were the first attempt by the Panther Party to establish a foothold in the South. Their operations demonstrated that the BPP was willing to become a truly national organization, but their efforts had failed by the middle of the 1970s.

Midwest Chapters

The midwestern chapters offer more examples of the difficulty local BPP organizers encountered when they began setting up their offices. The Chicago BPP began in August 1968 when two former SNCC organizers, Bob Brown and Bobby Rush, joined with Fred Hampton. The branch also united with another group of Chicago youth interested in forming a party office. Together they formed the first recognized party chapter.[33]

Fred Hampton was a former youth leader for the Maywood, Illinois, branch of the NAACP. The Chicago Panthers, under deputy chairman Fred Hampton's leadership, quickly became one of the most dynamic and inventive chapters in the national structure. Hampton mobilized hundreds of members and supporters to work in liberation schools, clothing programs, a medical clinic, and breakfast programs.[34] The branch fed approximately four thousand children daily at a network of sites on the south and west sides of Chicago. Black and white businesspeople supported them in their community outreach programs.[35]

The Chicago BPP began the original rainbow coalition in the spring of 1969. They allied with the Puerto Rican Young Lords Party and the white Young Patriot Party.[36] Both ethnic organizations respected the BPP and accepted its leadership.[37] The Panther Party believed that the coalition was a concrete demonstration of their ability to unite across racial lines to institute a far-reaching social revolution.

The BPP had less success when it attempted to persuade the Students for a Democratic Society (SDS) not to engage in a series of street demonstrations called the "Days of Rage." The demonstrations were intended to convince white radicals to revolt against the government. The SDS argued that these tactics would help to bring about the second American Revolution. Hampton told the SDS leaders their plan would only increase police repression, especially in the black community. The Panther leader also argued that the students should spend more time in educating white workers. The workers believed that the SDS, not the government, was their enemy. Hampton was ignored, and the demonstrations were repulsed.[38]

The BPP also attempted to reduce crime in the black community by politically educating Chicago's powerful gangs. The FBI undermined the effort. The government sent anonymous letters to the Blackstone Rangers and the BPP that accused the other of bad faith. The letters created and fueled an animosity between the two camps and convinced the Blackstone Rangers to attack the BPP. There were several subsequent clashes between the Rangers and Panthers.[39] The party had more success with the Black Disciples, who were convinced by the party to begin a breakfast program that fed 150 children.[40]

In the final analysis the BPP's gang outreach failed for two reasons. The first was the gangs' financial self-interest. Crime paid very well in Chicago. As long as the gangs kept away from politics, the police would apparently stay out of most of their affairs. The second reason was government interference via the counterintelligence program.

The government was evidently more comfortable with and preferred crime to an organized and politically conscious black community. Mayor Richard J. Daley and the police department refused to allow any opposition to the status quo in Chicago.

The Chicago Panthers had a series of violent confrontations with police in 1969. Police officers raided Panther headquarters in July after claiming they saw several individuals carrying weapons in front of the office. A gun battle occurred that resulted in several arrests, the loss of many supplies for the survival programs, and injuries to several police officers and Panthers. Another gun battle took place in October, when police responded to what they said was sniper fire coming from the roof of party headquarters. A policeman was wounded, and several Panthers were arrested. A shootout in November resulted in two police and one Panther killed. One Panther and several police officers were also wounded.[41]

The climax was reached in December when police raided a Panther apartment in the early morning hours while the occupants were asleep. Fred Hampton and Mark Clark (head of the Peoria branch) were killed. Four Panthers and two police officers were wounded.[42]

Police claimed the raid was the result of illegal weapons being stored at the apartment. A subsequent investigation showed, however, that the guns were legally registered. The coroner's jury returned a verdict of justifiable homicide, but the black community and the BPP refused to be satisfied with the decision. The NAACP, the SCLC, and the Chicago Afro-American Patrolman's League protested what they called an obvious murder.[43]

Further investigation revealed that William O' Neal, the Panther security chief, was an FBI informant who had supplied the police with an apartment floor plan and collected a three hundred dollar reward for his services. O'Neal committed suicide in 1990.[44] The survivors collected a judgment thirteen years after the deadly raid.

Bobby Rush led the Chicago chapter after Hampton's death. Rush and other Chicago Panthers also worked on Seale's election campaign, but Newton expelled Rush from the party after the election. The Chicago office had dwindled to seven members by 1977. The once-active Chicago office was closed in 1979.[45]

The Kansas City BPP had a brief but intense existence. Pete O'Neal and William Whitfield opened the chapter in January 1969. More than seven hundred people attended the first rally. The group attempted to have armed patrols monitoring the police in the spring of 1969, but a series of arrests and confrontations prompted a change of tactics.[46]

The BPP and O'Neal began a campaign in June 1969 to "expose" the Kansas City police chief for allegedly transferring weapons to a right-wing militia group called the Minutemen. An assassination attempt was made on O'Neal in the fall of 1969. The Panthers maintained that the police were responsible but were unable to offer convincing evidence. O'Neal and other members went to Washington, D.C., to testify before the House Committee on Internal Security and made their charges about the police chief with no result.[47]

The Kansas City chapter had more success with its breakfast and clothing programs and a medical clinic. The chapter also staged a "People's Demonstration against Filth" protest at city hall to complain about a new city ordinance that prohibited residential areas from burning trash. The Panthers maintained that the ordinance led to unsanitary conditions in the black community. Despite these programs the chapter was unable to sustain its cohesion when O'Neal fled to Algeria in 1970 after being charged with weapons violations. Membership dropped without his leadership, and the office was closed later that year.[48]

Pete O'Neal and his wife, Charlotte, relocated to Tanzania after leaving Algeria. Today O'Neal is the founder and managing director of the United African American Community Center in Arusha, Tanzania. In 2002 O'Neal and former Panther Geronimo Pratt concluded a successful project to bring water to the Tanzanian village of Imbaseni through Pratt's Kuji Foundation. The village now has a reliable source of water for the first time. This simple improvement has greatly enhanced the agriculture and health prospects of the entire area.[49]

The Detroit BPP began in 1967 but became inactive shortly afterward and had no members or finances. National organizers were sent in 1969 to reinvigorate the chapter as an NCCF, establish community programs, and sell newspapers. The Detroit office had three sites for breakfast programs and liberation schools and appeared to be committed to community organizing.[50]

An incident that occurred in October 1970 quickly changed the picture, however. Detroit police confronted two NCCF members who were supposedly coercing pedestrians into buying the newspaper. A crowd of bystanders intervened, and the NCCF personnel escaped to their nearby headquarters. Shots were fired from the office, and a policeman was killed. Fifteen NCCF members surrendered after a nine-hour siege that was mediated by community leaders and a black reporter. The confrontation curtailed much of the chapter's effectiveness, but it was still selling a small number of papers as late as 1979 before closing its doors.[51]

Western Chapters

Aaron Dixon began the Seattle chapter in March 1968. The Free Huey movement's hyperbole and heated rhetoric had a heavy influence on the chapter. Throughout 1968 Seattle featured a variety of paramilitary activities, such as target practice with live ammunition, first aid, and guerilla warfare instruction.

The national office ended these practices in 1969, and Seattle began operating three free-breakfast programs in November. By 1971 the breakfasts fed more than six hundred children daily, and a medical clinic made diagnoses and referrals to larger facilities.[52]

Peak membership in Seattle, however, coincided with the paramilitary activities and declined with community service. Paramilitary activities had attracted thirty members and more than two hundred supporters. Community service functions attracted eight to fifteen members.[53] Nevertheless, by this time, the national office was determined to eliminate overt paramilitary functions because the practice was too hazardous.

National headquarters was content with a smaller, more manageable membership that could sell one thousand papers a week, forward the funds to Oakland, and sustain survival programs such as the chapter's 1973 Thanksgiving Day feast. Political maturity had confirmed the knowledge that the quality of the membership and a consistent message of service were more conducive to organizational survival than large numbers of undisciplined Panthers.[54]

Vanetta Molson was fairly typical of the Seattle Panthers who joined after the chapter began to concentrate on survival programs. Molson was twenty-one and had previously worked with the Urban League in Columbia, South Carolina, where she had attempted to organize community and recreational centers. Molson considered her efforts in South Carolina to be a failure because poverty and health problems kept the children from studying. She returned to Seattle and attended community college before joining the BPP. Molson's duties consisted of working in the breakfast program, selling newspapers, and working in the free medical clinic. She took pride in her work because the community programs were "making our people strong so they could survive."[55] The Panthers were successfully recruiting a new kind of disciplined member interested in providing service to the community.

Alprentice "Bunchy" Carter founded the Southern California chapter in March 1968 and became deputy minister of defense. The Los Angeles BPP functioned in a city whose police force had traditionally been very aggressive toward blacks. The police department's metro squad was especially brutal and attempted to intimidate Panthers with beatings and illegal detentions. Carter was a prison friend of Eldridge Cleaver and a former member of the Slauson street gang. These circumstances were a critical influence on the chapter because Carter also began the chapter's military underground, which was kept separate from the regular party organization.[56]

Violent confrontations with Ron Karenga's ultranationalist US organization also influenced the party to adopt a military posture. The Panthers were embroiled in a political and territorial dispute with the US organization almost from the inception of the chapter. Karenga's group outnumbered the Panthers, and Carter ordered his people not to confront their opponents openly. US continued to provoke the Panthers by displaying weapons and employing occasional gang-style attacks (see chapter 4 for a more complete discussion of the BPP-US confrontations).

Geronimo Pratt, a Vietnam veteran who had been recruited by Carter, began an intensive program to defend the members from police attacks. Pratt turned the main Panther office into a virtual fortress that successfully withstood an attack in December 1969. The Panthers inside the office eventually had to surrender, but they managed to avoid being killed.

Part of the reason the Panthers were not harmed was because an outraged black community appeared in the surrounding streets. They demanded that the police allow the Panthers to surrender without being shot. The successful defense improved party morale after the deaths of Mark Clark and Fred Hampton, and Pratt's military reputation also increased.

The BPP began a free clinic, political support groups, and a prison-busing program, but the political environment was still dangerous because of the government's hostile approach to the party. The increased surveillance made it impossible for Pratt to operate openly, and he went underground in 1970. The Southern California chapter was deeply involved in the 1971 split. A courtroom skirmish between Pratt and Newton supporters revealed the depth of divided loyalties in the schism. The central committee eventually won the battle. Pratt's expulsion and Newton's suspicion of any dissension combined to limit the chapter's influence after 1971.

The San Quentin branch of the Panther Party was perhaps the most unique chapter. The members were all prisoners who theoretically were under state control at all times. Despite their handicaps they had a major influence on the BPP and the American Left. The San Quentin branch had its origins in the African American community's long and contentious involvement with the legal establishment.

The nineteenth-century abolitionists and the modern civil rights movement politicized resistance to unjust laws. Both movements invoked a higher moral authority to encourage disobedience to slavery and Jim Crow while simultaneously calling for the repeal of oppressive statutes. The BPP raised this tradition to new levels.

The Panthers reached into the jails and politicized the incarceration of ordinary people by asserting that these individuals had not received fair trials. In the Panther worldview, only an all-black jury could render a fair trial. The Panther Party viewed this strategy as heightening the contradictions already inherent between blacks and the legal system with the ultimate goal of overthrowing the current laws and replacing them with an as yet undefined revolutionary code.

The Nation of Islam pioneered the convict recruitment strategy when Elijah Muhammad was imprisoned during World War II for sedition and draft evasion. Muhammad maintained that blacks were not citizens and had no obligation to defend a country that had historically oppressed them. The fact that Muhammad was imprisoned is not the most significant aspect of his conviction, however.[57]

After all, the government was determined to prevent any undermining of the war effort regardless of whether or not it was conducted under religious auspices. Still, the curiosity Muhammad engendered among other black inmates made him aware that prison could be a fertile recruiting ground for the NOI. Enough black inmates attended Muhammad's services to attract the guards attention.[58]

Convicts were looking for some meaning to their life, and Muhammad was only too willing to provide answers to their questions. Muhammad began a regular correspondence with inmates after his release in 1946. His name and message spread throughout the convict community until it reached Malcolm Little.

Malcolm's rise to prominence within the NOI and his subsequent fame in the civil rights community were highly significant. Malcolm's personal ethics and self-discipline in pursuit of freedom proved that ex-convicts could make a contribution to the civil rights movement. Unfortunately for the movement, Malcolm's success story provided cover for other, less-ethical prisoners who also claimed his legacy.

The sad fact is that many of them were not capable of matching his ethical principles, contributions, or intellect. Unfortunately, as time proved, these negative matters were not likely to be discovered until the poseurs had already done their damage.

Newton and Seale, like the Nation of Islam, held their organization's doors open for ex-convicts. Former prisoners were diligently recruited throughout the party's history. This is easy to understand because Newton, Seale, and Cleaver were all incarcerated at some point. Furthermore, many of the party's first re-cruits were very familiar with the legal system because Newton and Seale fo-cused their efforts on the underclass, a group that tended to have run-ins with legal authorities.

Many of the young Panthers believed in the redemptive nature of the hu-man rights struggle. They had only to point to Malcolm X to make their case. The Panthers were not so naïve, however, as to believe that all prisoners were created equal. They initially divided the prison population into two categories: regular and political. Regular prisoners were men and women with little or no political awareness. They were incarcerated for the usual criminal offenses.

Political prisoners were Panthers and other radicals who were jailed for ac-tivities connected to their political beliefs. The government's relentless offen-sive against the BPP generated a seemingly endless list of candidates for po-litical prisoner status: Newton, Seale, the New York 21 (who were charged with a bombing conspiracy), the New Haven 14 (who were charged with killing a suspected informer), and others too numerous to mention. Political prisoners also included convicts whose consciousness had been raised during their incar-ceration and who subsequently joined the BPP.

George Jackson was perhaps the most famous and influential prisoner in this category. Jackson had robbed a gas station when he was eighteen and received an indeterminate prison term of one year to life. This sentence meant that his suitability for parole would be reviewed on a regular basis, and recommendations would be based on his behavior, that is, not being a discipline problem. Under this system prisoners would enroll in recommended psychological and educational programs that were designed to gain release regardless of whether any real benefit was obtained. Convicts referred to this as programming. Jackson did not follow the program.[59]

He advocated for black inmates and organized them against other ethnic factions and the prison administration. Prison authorities continually delayed his release. He spent more than seven years in various forms of solitary confinement and became more radical with each passing day. Jackson claimed that the prison authorities had tried to assassinate him more than twenty times either through the guards or by bribing white inmates.[60]

The Panther Party's politics had a great influence on Jackson. He believed that the BPP was the most powerful political force outside of establishment politics. Jackson began to preach that the revolution was also taking place inside the correctional institutions. Jackson and others attempted the long-term process of transforming the black criminal mentality into a black revolutionary mentality.[61]

This message found a receptive audience among California's growing prison population. The men lived in extreme conditions, and some of them began to compare their situation to guerilla fighters. Their living conditions also inculcated a willingness to use violence to further their objectives. Hardened and disciplined, they seemed to be ideal soldiers for a revolutionary movement. The Panther Party, in a bid to control and guide the burgeoning prison movement, called for a clear linkage between the BPP and prison organizations.

Imprisoned Panthers began to refer to themselves as prisoners of war and maintained that "there was an indisputable relationship between the political prisoner and the people in the street."[62] Many Panthers believed they would eventually be freed through their own efforts or a negotiated settlement that would be forced on the government.

The use of the terms "political prisoner" and "prisoner of war" was highly significant. The phrases indicated a completely different condition from common criminals. "Political prisoner" signified a higher status for Panthers and the struggle they represented. "Prisoner-of-war" status meant they considered themselves as soldiers in a war against the government. This term also gave them psychological comfort. POW status meant they were not separated from struggles waged outside the walls.[63]

In 1970 three black convicts were killed in a racial fight in the Soledad prison exercise yard. A prison guard was slain in retaliation after a grand jury returned a verdict of justifiable homicide in the convicts' death. George Jackson, Fleeta Drumgo, and John Cluchette were charged with the guard's murder.[64]

Jackson and his cohorts became known as the Soledad Brothers. They became well known in radical circles around the world when Jackson's prison letters and essays were published in 1970 and 1971. The BPP, numerous sympathizers, and a young college professor named Angela Davis rallied to the Soledad Brothers' defense. Jackson was transferred to San Quentin to stand trial at the Marin County courthouse in Northern California.

Tragedy struck in August 1970 when Jackson's younger brother, Jonathan, 17, smuggled guns to three inmates (Ruchell Magee, Willie Christmas, and James McClain) while they were in Marin County to give testimony in an unrelated trial. Jonathan Jackson's goal was to reach a radio station, where he would demand the release of his brother and a plane to fly out of the country. Judge Harold Haley, District Attorney Gary Thomas, and jurors Maria Graham, Joyce Rodom, and Doris Wagner were taken as hostages. The whole group attempted to flee in a van from the courthouse parking lot. Prison guards and sheriffs, however, exchanged fire with Jackson and his friends. Judge Haley, Jackson, Christmas, and McClain were killed. District Attorney Thomas and juror Wagner were wounded. The remaining two jurors were unharmed. Ruchell Magee was the only surviving inmate.[65]

A subsequent investigation resulted in an indictment against Angela Davis for allegedly providing the weapons used in the attempted breakout. Davis, however, denied all knowledge of the plot. She said that Jackson had taken the guns without her knowledge, and then she went underground to evade prosecution. She was captured later that year but acquitted at her trial. Ruchell Magee was tried and convicted. He is currently serving a life sentence in the California Department of Corrections.

In February 1971 the BPP revealed the existence of a party branch at San Quentin under the leadership of George Jackson. Six months later Jackson, along with several other prisoners and guards, was killed during another escape attempt. Authorities claimed the elaborate escape attempt was supposed to take place at night after the prison's electricity was short-circuited. The inmates were then supposed to break out of maximum security and use rope ladders to climb the walls and reach waiting jeeps. A visitor allegedly supplied Jackson with a gun on August 21, 1971. The weapon was seen when he was being searched after returning to the maximum security adjustment center. Jackson then pulled the gun, released several prisoners, and took six guards hostage.

The prisoners killed three guards, Sergeant Jere Graham, Frank DeLeon, and Paul Krasner, and two white inmates, John Lynn and Ronald Kane. Three other guards, Urbano Rubiaco, Charles Breckenridge, and Kenneth McCray, were wounded. The authorities outside the cellblock were alerted by this time and surrounded the area. Jackson ran from the adjustment center to draw the guards' fire. He was killed instantly, and the attempt collapsed.

Jackson's death prompted many conspiracy theories about how the government had provoked an escape and then killed him during the attempt.[66] A female Panther with supposed ties to the government was alleged to have passed a tape recorder (with a pistol hidden in it) to Jackson. No warrant was ever issued to investigate the allegation, however. The woman has denied all knowledge of a plot, and neither the prosecution nor defense called her to testify in any trial stemming from the escape attempt. No conclusive proof has ever been offered to verify the charges. The full truth of Jackson's death remains a mystery.[67]

Eastern Chapters

The New York BPP was founded in 1968. The chapter began in Brooklyn and expanded to the Bronx, Corona, Harlem, Jamaica, and Washington Heights. Branches outside of New York City were located in Albany, Buffalo, Mount Vernon, and Peekskill. The New York City Panthers, like other chapters, originally emphasized the Free Huey campaign. The chapter was founded at a time when the local black community was also waging an intense political struggle to control its own institutions. The Panther community-control program dovetailed with this larger campaign. Panthers worked with other organizers in Brooklyn's Ocean Hill–Brownsville neighborhood for community control of schools and circulated petitions for decent housing.[68]

When the party began a breakfast for schoolchildren, New York City had several sites featuring the full array of survival programs. In a burst of revolutionary zeal the Brooklyn branch seized an abandoned building used for the drug trade and converted it to a community information center with a health clinic and a breakfast program. The New York City chapter was also instrumental in contributing to party revenues through its sales of the *Black Panther*. During one period in 1969 the chapter sold one-third of the entire national circulation and sent $13,000 to national headquarters.[69]

In April 1969 the New York City chapter was rocked by a series of raids. The district attorney alleged that the Panthers were plotting to bomb police stations, railroads, department stores, and the Bronx Botanical Gardens. Twenty-one Panthers were indicted and fifteen arrested on a variety of charges, which ranged from conspiracy to commit murder and arson to possession of explosives.

Many of the arrested Panthers had been involved with the founding of the chapter. Their loss meant that national headquarters had to send in organizers from California who were unfamiliar with the community's political history and cultural nuances.[70] The California Panthers clashed with the New York members over the outward manifestations of cultural nationalism. The New York Panthers saw no contradiction between being in the party and flying the red, black, and green flag of African nationalism.

These practices caused problems because the central committee frowned on these cultural displays.[71] The California Panthers were also very heavy-handed in demanding that the chapter concentrate on survival programs and on selling newspapers to the exclusion of organizing on other issues, such as housing. The New York Panthers began to believe the national office did not appreciate them as political organizers and believed they were only useful for fund-raising.

The chapter did manage to bail out two members of the New York 21. They were Richard "Dharuba" Moore and Michael "Cetawayo" Tabor. These men were able to articulate the chapter's grievances. Moore and Tabor also chafed at the central committee's unwillingness to listen to the regional office's policy suggestions.[72]

The New York Panthers believed that the national headquarters should allow the local branches to keep more of their newspaper money to help support prisoners and to upgrade living conditions for the rank and file. Moreover, they wanted the authority to begin local initiatives to explore improving community conditions. They objected to spending so much of their time selling newspapers. The New York Panthers saw themselves as true community organizers and not just paper sellers or social workers. In addition, they were shocked when Newton and the central committee began to abandon even a rhetorical commitment to armed struggle (see chapter 4).

Other New York Panthers charged that a majority of party funds were being used to support the leadership's legal cases while local members were left to their own devices. The New York 21 openly criticized the national leadership. Zayd Shakur, deputy minister of information, unsuccessfully attempted to mediate the mushrooming dispute, and a majority of the members of the New York chapter became increasingly disillusioned and bitter over their treatment.[73]

The central committee expelled the New York 21. This move convinced many in the chapter that their comrades had been cynically exploited to raise money for national headquarters and then cast aside when they attempted to criticize the party's new direction.

Eldridge Cleaver and the New York chapter became allies in the fight to oppose Newton and his loyalists. The schism forced Tabor and Moore underground because they feared the government and Newton's wrath. The counterintelligence program not only took advantage of the party's confusion but also continued to create turmoil with forged letters and constant rumor mongering. The New York 21 were acquitted in May 1971 after a nine-month trial, but Tabor and Moore remained underground.[74]

The 1971 schism brought about the downfall of Newton loyalists in New York and the rise of an alternative BPP. The dissidents wanted to establish what they considered to be a truly revolutionary organization with separate political and military wings. The militants went underground to become guerillas. Dissidents argued that the community should be educated about the necessity of armed struggle through political work and survival programs. They did not believe, however, in the static defense of Panther offices that resulted in only more prisoners and high legal costs. Dissidents advocated the use of mobile, urban guerillas to defeat the government. The militants began to refer to themselves as the Black Liberation Army (BLA). Their operations were called armed propaganda.[75]

The aboveground organization printed the newspaper *Right On!* The journal acted as a conduit between urban guerillas and the community. The militants, however, failed to analyze the political situation objectively. The government's overwhelming power and the militants' own organizational missteps defeated them. This did not happen, however, until six BLA members and eight police officers had been killed. One of the dead was New York chapter leader Zayd Shakur.[76]

Right On! continued to publish until 1974, but the New York Panthers never recovered from the split. For that matter, neither did the regular party. Neither Newton nor the dissidents were able to rebuild an effective organization in the nation's largest city.

The Philadelphia chapter began in late 1968 with a membership that ranged from eight to ten members. Philadelphia had a long history of community activism, and many black organizations were located there. The NAACP, CORE, the Republic of New Africa, the SCLC, the Revolutionary Action Movement, and the Young Black Alliance represented a broad spectrum of political thought, ranging from integrationists to Black Nationalists. Despite this political involvement, local party members were ineffective until national organizers arrived in October 1969.

The chapter was reinvigorated, and by September 1970 several breakfast programs, liberation schools, and a Mark Clark Free Health Care Clinic had been organized. Local police estimated that membership ranged from eighty to one hundred Panthers located at three offices in north and south Philadelphia.[77]

The most well-known event in the chapter's history was the 1970 Revolutionary People's Constitutional Convention. The weekend before the RPCC was to start, there were two attacks on the Philadelphia police by black radicals who were non-Panthers. The Philadelphia police were commanded by Pete Rizzo, who was well known on the East Coast for his aggressive tactics, especially against the black community.

The police arrested the perpetrators, and for good measure they also raided the three party offices and arrested fourteen Panthers. Three policemen were wounded at one location by shotgun fire, but there were no other casualties. The police confiscated a dozen weapons and a large quantity of ammunition along with party literature. The raid became notorious because the police made the male Panthers strip naked in the street under the pretense of searching for weapons. Chief Rizzo claimed the police had received intelligence about illegal weapons, but he could not explain why they waited to attack the BPP until non-Panthers shot officers.[78]

The Panthers believed that the police were trying to disrupt the convention, but the RPCC proceeded anyway. The convention was remarkably peaceful despite the previous dramatic events. The SDS, the Weathermen, the Gay Liberation Front, the Women's Liberation Front, the Society of Friends, and many unaffiliated individuals came to hear speeches by Newton and Michael Tabor. Workshops covered a variety of social and political issues, but a great deal of controversy existed about what had actually been accomplished. Most participants did not believe any concrete movement toward a new constitution had been made. At least 40 percent of the participants were whites. This disturbed many Panthers and other blacks.[79]

There were several reasons why so few black activists were involved. The International Congress of African Peoples was held in Atlanta at the same time as the RPCC. The meeting was billed as Pan-African and nationalist, but moderate civil rights groups also attended.[80]

Furthermore, many black organizations disagreed with the BPP's claim to be the vanguard of the struggle. They disparaged alliances with nonblack organizations and criticized the Panther's Marxist philosophy as detrimental to black people. Black Nationalists in particular and the black community in general had difficulty integrating Marxism into the black experience. Marxists had traditionally urged black-white unity for a class struggle. Most blacks resisted because they did not believe racism would disappear because of a proletarian victory.

In fact, there was an objective basis for black distrust. The Communist Party of the United States had vigorously attacked Marcus Garvey and the Universal Negro Improvement Association. They argued that his program of selective immigration to Liberia would distract blacks from struggling for political power in the United States. The Communists had recruited American blacks during the Great Depression, promising equal treatment and a voice in party affairs. Black writers such as Richard Wright later resigned from the Communist Party after concluding they had been manipulated for propaganda purposes.[81]

The national hunt for Communists during the McCarthy era confirmed the inherent dangers of Marxism for many blacks. Alarm bells went off in the black community when the BPP began to articulate a Marxist analysis of American society. Most activists were also aware that the Panther gathering was more likely to attract police repression than the International Congress of African Peoples. All in all, there were more than enough reasons for many black organizations to go to Atlanta rather than Philadelphia.

The Philadelphia chapter, like other offices, lost membership during the schism. There were only twelve hundred papers sold in July 1972, and the central committee ordered all remaining offices closed in 1977.[82]

Erika Huggins founded the New Haven, Connecticut, chapter in January 1969. She had come to bury her husband in his hometown. Jon Huggins had been killed by the US organization in Los Angeles. (Chapter 4 has a more complete discussion of these events.) Several community members approached Erika Huggins and asked her to form a BPP chapter in New Haven. National headquarters directed Huggins to join with a previously existing chapter in Bridgeport. The chapter soon relocated to New Haven and took the Bridgeport members along. Membership ranged from fifteen to twenty-five people at this time.[83]

From 1969 to 1971 New England was the scene of one of the most confusing and costly affairs in Panther history. Bobby Seale and several other Panthers were arrested and charged with the kidnapping, torture, and murder of another party member.

The Panthers denied all charges and maintained that the murder was committed by an agent provocateur. The case was used as an excuse by police agencies to raid offices all across the country in an alleged search for fugitives connected to the murder. Seale and another codefendant were eventually freed of all charges, though other Panthers were convicted.

The Connecticut chapter was formed when the central committee was trying to weed out informers and undisciplined members. Intensified PE classes and a ban on recruiting were two instruments of this policy. Internal party politics provided an opening for the FBI to sow havoc.

The New Haven chapter was visited in May by a former California Panther named George Sams. Sams claimed the central committee had sent him to purge the chapter of informers. He had previously been in New York but had left hurriedly after learning an authentic central committee representative was on the way. Alex Rackley, a New York Panther, accompanied Sams to New Haven.[84]

Sams turned on Rackley for unknown reasons and accused him of being an informant. Rackley was held and tortured for three days by Sams and other members of the New Haven chapter. Landon Williams and Rory Hithe, official representatives of the central committee, visited New Haven at this juncture. Bobby Seale followed them shortly thereafter. Seale was scheduled to speak at Yale as part of a nationwide fund-raising tour. Williams, Seale, and Hithe discovered Rackley was being tortured. Seale said that at this point he ordered the prisoner to be released. Shortly afterward, Williams, Hithe, and Seale left town.[85]

Sams and four other Panthers took Rackley to an isolated spot and murdered him. A nationwide investigation ensued. Seale was arrested in California. Williams and Hithe were arrested in Denver. Sams and another Panther were apprehended in Salt Lake City. Huggins and seven others were arrested in New Haven. The case was initially a serious blow to the New Haven BPP because only five members were left to keep the office open.[86]

The central committee sent reinforcements and made the city an example of community involvement. The chapter opened a breakfast program, community political education, and a free clothing program by January of 1970. Newton visited the prisoners in 1971 after he was freed. Seale and Huggins were freed in 1971 after a mistrial. They returned to California, and the New Haven chapter functioned until the mid-seventies, when it was closed.

International Involvement

The BPP also waged a vigorous campaign to influence international opinion. Kathleen Cleaver went to Japan in 1968 to protest against American military policies in the Far East. The then minister of education, George Murray, also visited Cuba, and Bobby Seale met Vietcong representatives at a Montreal Hemispheric Conference to end the Vietnam War.[87]

International involvement intensified when Eldridge Cleaver fled the United States for Cuba in 1968 to avoid incarceration for parole violations stemming from his involvement in a gun battle with Oakland police. Cuba had also sheltered the fugitive Robert Williams. Williams resided there until 1965 and was allowed to broadcast a program called *Radio Free Dixie*. He also published the *Crusader* newsletter, which was clandestinely circulated in the United States.

The Cubans originally supported Williams because they believed that African Americans could be a divisive force in the United States. They changed the policy later because of their internal political situation.[88] Afro-Cubans made up at least 30 percent of the population, and the island was plagued with long-standing racial discrimination issues. The Cuban government came to believe that support for Black Nationalist self-determination was fine in the United

States, but a similar movement in Cuba would adversely affect Castro's plan to integrate the island under Marxism.[89]

American radicals arranged for Cleaver's Cuban stay, but the visit was plagued from the start by misunderstandings and international politics. Cleaver wanted to use Cuba as a political base against the United States. This request was denied. The Cuban government wanted to keep secret the nature of its involvement with black militants. Consequently, the government demanded that Cleaver live as a private citizen with minimal publicity.[90]

Nevertheless, Reuters reported Cleaver's presence in May 1969, and his asylum became increasingly untenable. The Cubans decided to eliminate their problem by reuniting Cleaver with his wife in Algeria and then transporting them to Jordan. Cleaver objected to the plan because he wanted to stay in Algeria as a representative of the BPP.

The Organization of African Unity had previously designated Algeria as the host country for all of Africa's liberation movements.[91] The Palestinian Liberation Organization, the Vietcong, the North Vietnamese, and other revolutionary groups also resided there.

Eldridge Cleaver's appearance at the 1969 Pan-African Cultural Festival put the American government on notice that he was active in Africa. Cleaver opened the BPP international section in 1970 when the Algerian government recognized the Panthers as the sole representative of the African American people.[92]

The Algiers office was responsible for publicizing the BPP on an international level, making alliances with other groups and countries, and lobbying the United Nations in behalf of black Americans. The international section also wanted to have a military training facility in Algeria, but this was denied. Despite this rebuff the international section was able to score some diplomatic successes.

The Panthers toured North Korea and North Vietnam in 1970, and the North Vietnamese staged an International Day of Solidarity with the Afro-American People on the anniversary of the 1965 Watts uprising. The high-profile visits served both parties' interests. The Koreans and Vietnamese advanced their own propaganda by offering a stage for American dissenters. Cleaver was able to broadcast to American troops, urging them to lay down their arms. The North Vietnamese also offered to exchange American prisoners of war for Huey Newton and Bobby Seale. The U.S. government ignored the proposal because it would have legitimized the BPP's revolutionary credentials as an alternative government.[93]

The international section was also a haven for other fugitives. Party members Don Cox and Pete and Charlotte O'Neal arrived by 1970. Not all fugitives were Panthers, however. Timothy Leary, the LSD guru, escaped a California prison and came to Algeria. Cleaver put Leary under "house arrest" in 1971 for drug use, but this high-handed action brought the international section into conflict with Algerian authorities.[94]

Cleaver's notoriety and belligerence also made him the natural rallying point for Panthers who were dissatisfied with Newton's plan to disengage from armed struggle. Michael "Cetawayo" Tabor and his wife, Connie Matthews, fled to Algeria in 1971. Their arrival intensified the party's internal struggles.

Cleaver issued a series of pronouncements encouraging military action to reclaim the "revolution" from the reformers. Bobby Rush contends that Cleaver called him after Fred Hampton's death in 1969 and urged Chicago Panthers to strike back against the police. Rush claims an attack was ordered prior to Cleaver's call but never happened. In hindsight the lack of any retaliation may have actually worked to the Panthers' benefit in allowing them to claim the moral high ground and educate the community. Rush remembers thinking how odd it was for Cleaver to suggest any military action from a villa in Algiers.[95]

Subsequent events in Algeria also showed that Cleaver had a dangerously inaccurate assessment of his position there as well. A series of airplane hijackings by black Americans demanding passage to Algeria had occurred. The hijackers had also received ransom money they said should be used for revolutionary purposes.

The Algerian government could not accept this plan because it was involved in a series of quiet and delicate negotiations with American companies to exploit the country's vast oil and gas reserves. The reserves were needed to develop the country. The Algerians believed that returning the ransom money was the only option that would secure their economic future.

The government quietly returned the aircraft and the ransom while handing the hijackers over to the Panthers. Cleaver responded by publishing an open letter to the Algerian president in the French newspaper *Le Monde*. The letter demanded that the ransom money be turned over to the Panthers and accused the government of defaulting on its revolutionary responsibilities.[96]

Cleaver's public criticism embarrassed the Algerians. It was also heedless because his political position was extremely weak. The Panthers were guests, and diplomatic recognition could easily be rescinded. The international section had no obvious benefit to its host besides being a nuisance to the U.S. government. Financial reality soon overrode that slight consideration.

The Algerian authorities closed the international section in August 1972, and the BPP staff began to leave. O'Neal and his wife went to a collective farm in Tanzania. Donald Cox published an open letter dissociating himself from the party. Other Panthers drifted away to unknown locations. Eldridge Cleaver returned to the United States in 1975 to face criminal charges stemming from his original flight. The revolutionary had returned home.[97]

The BPP international section fulfilled Malcolm X's dream of winning diplomatic recognition for black Americans. The political reality, however, failed to meet radical expectations. The Panthers were aided by worldwide dissatisfaction with America's Vietnam policy. This created the temporary illusion of unity with a variety of groups that objectively did not have much in common with African Americans.

The Panthers believed they were allied with the wretched of the earth. There were, however, major differences in political, material, and social conditions between the United States and the third world. Panthers came from the richest and most technologically advanced society in history. Despite acknowledged disadvantages, African Americans still had access to a standard of living that was completely unavailable to a majority of the world's people.

Panther political values were ultimately American regardless of a professed allegiance to Marxism. By 1972 the BPP had turned its back on armed struggle. It began to speak of working within the existing political system to achieve full democratic and political rights for African Americans. On the other hand, most third-world and socialist countries were governed by one-party regimes with little or no regard for Western concepts of democracy.

Unfortunately, the Panther Party entered international politics armed with little more than moral authority. Cuba and Algeria taught the Panthers that naked self-interest was the determining factor between governments and exile organizations. The international section was well treated when it suited the interests of Algeria or Cuba.

The end of the Vietnam War, however, ended a major source of international dissatisfaction with the United States. It also transformed Communist and third-world flirtation with American internal dissent. They no longer treated domestic organizations as liberation movements. The BPP was a dissident faction that could embarrass the American government but obviously had no chance of overthrowing it.

Some former Panthers are still unable to return to the United States. Pete O'Neal faces weapons charges from 1970 that the government will not dismiss. Don Cox is wanted for questioning about his alleged activities in the BLA.

These men have paid a heavy price for being totally committed to what they believed was a revolution. They and the international section are casualties of that particular time and place.

Evaluating the Chapters

Regional branches were more successful when they responded to local conditions. Patrolling the police or openly carrying weapons (as occurred in Oakland) could not be duplicated without great cost because the police adapted to the tactics. Fred Hampton opposed the Weathermen because he believed their "Days of Rage" would only increase police repression in the black community and anger potential white allies.

Hampton was right. Chicago, Kansas City, and Detroit achieved their greatest successes with survival programs. Grassroots organizing, not guns, attracted more community support. On the other hand, police repression was unabated no matter what approach the regional branches used.

Panther chapters always had to contend with a hostile political environment. Police departments were determined to keep the BPP from gaining a foothold in their communities. The Chicago BPP was perhaps more involved in community organizing than any other branch. Yet the police killed Fred Hampton precisely because they feared his organizing skills.

The BPP encountered unrelieved police hostility everywhere, whether it was Boston, North Carolina, New Orleans, Los Angeles, or Baltimore. Party organizers were certain that beatings and detentions were the least they could hope for whether they advocated community programs or attacks on police.

It is nothing short of amazing that local Panthers were able to accomplish as much as they did, given their relative inexperience, resource scarcity, and government enmity. Local communities produced outstanding and intelligent organizers in every region without exception. Examples include Fred Hampton and Mark Clark in Illinois, Bobby Hutton in Oakland, Zayd Shakur in New York, and Edwin (Breeze) Barrow in Jersey City.

These men and women were courageous, intelligent, and innovative leaders. They managed to institute survival programs and build relations with other community groups while under enormous pressure. The Panthers learned their organizing lessons in the hard school of the streets. They gained a wealth of experience if they survived. Many of the regional leaders believed they should have been given central committee membership, and they had a strong case.

Regional membership was a logical step and would have broadened the central committee's experience and political outlook. New ideas on a wide range of topics would have been available. For instance, there was an inordinate and unnecessary amount of secrecy concerning financial matters. Regional branches resented having to request their own money for local initiatives.

They reasoned that the funds had been raised through their own hard work and that they should receive due consideration about how the money was to be spent. The New York 21 and other prisoners argued that they were not receiving a fair share of the money being allotted for legal expenses.

Whether or not this was true misses the point. Some Panthers believed it was true, and that perception became reality. Newton's 1971 move to copyright the *Black Panther* confirmed many people's fears. This legal move turned a cooperative effort into a private enterprise. Party finances were increasingly centralized.[99]

Ordinary members came to believe that the central committee misappropriated funds, and this was a key source of dissatisfaction. The FBI's rumor mill willingly contributed to the known facts about the central committee's financial arrangements.

Stipends were not issued to every member until 1979, when it was too late. In the final analysis the Oakland-based leadership was simply unwilling to share decision making or financial responsibility. The regional members were simply supposed to carry out orders.

BPP membership was highest in 1968 when the Free Huey campaign was at its peak. The party, however, was most effective from 1969 through Seale's election campaign, when it had a smaller but more dedicated cadre of workers. Part of the effectiveness was due to the community programs, but the main reason was the morale of the rank and file. Ordinary members withstood deadly challenges from the government and the stresses of party life because they believed in their political message.

Power became more concentrated in Oakland after 1971 because opponents and rivals were purged. Furthermore, Seale's campaign brought about the demise of many thriving local branches when members were transferred to Oakland to work in electoral politics. Many leaders objected to this move, but Newton overruled them. There was no viable political reason to close these chapters for the 1973 election campaign.

Regional branches responded to local needs. Panthers committed to their communities staffed them. The effectiveness of local organizations had been validated. Given time, perhaps the communities would have taken over the survival programs. This would have freed the Panthers to undertake other more-demanding tasks. The offices that escaped being closed had only four more years to operate.

In August 1977 the central committee decided that all remaining chapters and branches would be closed within two months.[100] Some branches, however, continued to sell newspapers through 1979, but their political base was greatly diminished.

The once-dynamic regional branches were closed because they lacked purpose and members. The people and conditions that allowed their creation were gone. The Panther Party returned to its Oakland roots, and the regional that once characterized the organization never returned.[101]

4

ENEMIES OF THE PEOPLE

But the simple fact is that neither the Black Panther Party nor any person who is part of it is above or beyond criticism....Those of us who constitute the extreme left wing of the Black Panther Party will continue to criticize whenever criticism is needed to expose counter-revolutionary acts.

—*Right On!,* April 1971

In 1971 the BPP's leaders startled the rank and file with a public quarrel over ideology and tactics while the organization was struggling with the government for its very life. This extraordinary development tore the Panther Party apart. Ordinary members were called on to declare their loyalty for one side or the other. These agonizing decisions would be based on their reasons for joining the Panthers, whether their expectations had been met, and what they thought the future held for them and the black community.

The BPP was changed forever by the 1971 schism that fractured the party. Panthers call this political breakup the "split." After 1971 the Panthers were no longer a self-proclaimed revolutionary organization advocating the overthrow of the American government. The BPP transitioned to a reform party that provided social services to the black community and worked for change within the existing political system.

The story of this transformation is one of pragmatism and miscalculation, sacrifice and opportunism, courage, fratricide, and Machiavellian government operations. Mostly, however, it is a story of how ordinary Panthers endured a situation not of their making.

The African American community, the radical wing of American politics, and an international audience watched as the Panthers engaged in a public battle over the correct way to organize the black community for social change. Party members who had struggled alongside each other for years became bitter enemies in 1971.

Dissidents derided as reformist the very community programs that had been the lifeblood of the party. The central committee was attacked for being reactionary, undemocratic, and morally corrupt.[1] Blood was spilled on both sides of the divide.

It was difficult for observers or participants to know all the facts as events unfolded with breathtaking speed. Many party members were confused as they struggled to make sense of the political and personal calamity that threatened to engulf their lives.

Panthers who were underground, jailed, or in exile were in great difficulty. They did not know what would become of their support if they chose the losing side. These men and women had sacrificed their future because they had believed in the party's political message. Their lives had been "transformed by an idea that had given meaning to their existence."[2] Now that same message was being disputed and fought over by their friends.

Many former Panthers still find it difficult to discuss the schism. They are convinced that the party and the black community never recovered from the traumatic events of 1971. The "split" is also a story still searching for the government's true role in the proceedings because all the relevant documents may not have been released.

Certain facts are not in dispute, however. The schism and the subsequent victory of the Newton loyalists were crucial to determining the future role of the BPP. The Panther Party never again confronted the government as they had from 1966 to 1971. Bobby Seale's 1973 Oakland mayoral campaign rested firmly on the path chosen in 1971.

A Party Torn Apart: 1971–1974

Party life existed on three interrelated levels from 1971 to 1974. The first level was the continued operation of the survival programs by the rank and Community programs exemplified the Panther message of social reform and had to be continued if the BPP was to retain any credibility within the black community. The second level was the tendency to address internal party disputes and contradictions with the community in a violent manner. The third level was the election campaign of Bobby Seale and Elaine Brown. The conflation of these activities delivered a mixed message to the community as the party endured the full spectrum of change and turmoil.

Problems became apparent during the winter of 1970–71 when Huey Newton began to implement ideological changes. The first change was heralded in a newspaper article titled "Survival Pending Revolution." The article was the official recognition of an obvious fact. The Panther Party's primary organizing method was to be the community programs, not armed force against the state. The BPP would henceforth "concentrate on the immediate needs of the people, in order to build a united political force.... Survival pending revolution is our immediate task."[3]

This was a radical departure for the Panthers, who had once expressed no qualms about being a revolutionary organization advocating armed resistance to the American government. The departure was so striking that it appeared to catch the paper's editorial staff off guard because the same issue included an insert that continued to advocate guerilla war in the United States.[4]

Political infighting over the change became public in January 1971 with the purge of Elmer "Geronimo" Pratt. This confrontation made it clear that some party militants wanted to continue the older policy of using military tactics to organize the black community. Pratt was the highly respected deputy defense minister from Southern California. He had been frequently lauded as an exemplar of revolutionary virtues.

Newton now claimed that Pratt had taken actions detrimental to organizational discipline. Pratt was accused of going underground and recruiting his own army to wage a personal war against the government. He and others were expelled for being a "counter-revolutionary little roving band" and violating discipline. The central committee also maintained that Pratt had threatened their lives when he was called on to explain his actions.[5]

Pratt's side of the story was different. He acknowledged that he was a fugitive from justice because of his failure to appear in court for a 1969 shootout with police. When he was arrested in Dallas in the winter of 1970, however, Pratt claimed that Newton had ordered him to go underground and then betrayed him to the police for unknown reasons.[6] Panthers were confused by these events. Later in 1971 they were stunned by a senseless tragedy: the brutal murder of Pratt's wife.

Sandra Pratt disappeared in November 1971 as she and her husband were standing trial in Los Angeles on weapons charges. The discovery of her nude, pregnant body precipitated a courtroom brawl between Pratt and his friends and Newton supporters. It was widely assumed (though never proved) in dissident circles that Newton was somehow responsible. Despite this speculation Sandra Pratt's killers were never found. Her death, though, added fuel to the smoldering fire of the Panther wars.[7]

Geronimo Pratt was ultimately convicted on weapons charges and an earlier murder. Pratt maintained that the murder charge was a false accusation. He spent twenty-five years in prison before his sentence was overturned and he was released in 1997.

Other events followed rapidly before Pratt's fall from grace could be absorbed. Newton expelled the entire leadership of the international section of the BPP, the New York chapter, and a group of celebrated prisoners known as the New York 21 for openly disagreeing with his leadership.

The New York 21 had written a letter to a New York City alternative newspaper criticizing Newton's ideological about-face and simultaneously praising the white Weather Underground. Newton and the central committee viewed the letter as a breach of discipline that could not be tolerated. The expulsion of the New York 21 followed quickly.[8]

Panthers knew Cleaver as "the Rage" for his advocacy of armed struggle to achieve national liberation for black Americans. Cleaver argued that the BPP should not confuse peaceful mass activities such as the community programs with the party's military objectives. Mass activities were to be used to attract political support and money. Cleaver believed, however, that the goal of national liberation could be achieved only by force. Consequently, he was at loggerheads with Newton over the party's new direction and Pratt's unexpected expulsion.[9]

Cleaver knew that Newton and Hilliard were changing the party's direction. His dissent became public on February 26, 1971, when a San Francisco television station invited Newton and Cleaver to discuss current affairs. Cleaver spoke to the audience via telephone from Algiers. He immediately began to demand that the central committee rescind the expulsion of Pratt and the New York 21.[10]

Cleaver also demanded the resignation or expulsion of the Hilliard brothers. He alleged that they were a negative influence on the party's ideology and practice. Cleaver chose not to confront Newton directly at that time. His reticence did not matter because four high-ranking New York Panthers (Michael "Cetewayo" Tabor; his wife, Connie Matthews; Richard "Dharuba" Moore; and Eddie "Jamal" Joseph) disappeared with important party documents. The four subsequently declared their loyalty to Cleaver.

The central committee believed they were organizing a dissident faction, and all four were expelled as "enemies of the people."[11] The Tabors went to Algiers and joined Cleaver, and Richard Moore and Eddie Joseph remained in New York. The central committee expelled Cleaver. For good measure it also accused him of holding his wife hostage and murdering her lover.[12]

Newton intensified the conflict by writing an essay for the party newspaper. According to Newton, while he was in jail the party had come under the malign influence of Cleaver and had strayed from its original vision. That vision had imagined the community survival programs and had called for armed struggle only as a temporary tactic to awaken the people to the seriousness of their plight.[13]

According to Newton, this temporary tactic had now outlived its usefulness. Newton charged that Cleaver wanted to continue pursuing an incorrect policy because he wanted power. Newton also argued that the black community's actions showed they did not support armed struggle. Consequently, it was time for the BPP to return to its original vision because any other choice was suicidal given the obvious disparity in forces.[14]

Newton now maintained that the struggle in America was political, not military. This was in spite of his well-known words and actions from 1966 to 1970. Newton managed to retain the loyalty of George Jackson, who led the San Quentin branch of the Panther Party. Jackson was very influential in radical circles because of his status as a charismatic and outspoken prison revolutionary. Jackson attacked Cleaver in extremely virulent terms, charging him with counterrevolution, and repeated Newton's accusation that Cleaver had killed an exiled fellow Panther.[15]

Jackson's support came at a crucial time for Newton. It helped to shield him from charges that he had betrayed the revolution. Panther dissidents countered that Newton was controlling Jackson's access to the true state of affairs in the BPP and that he was not responsible for his words. These tactics sought to nullify Jackson's words without attacking him and arousing public anger against the dissidents.

Meanwhile, the party's underground military wing, the Black Liberation Army, defied Newton and continued to pursue guerilla war in an effort to achieve a national uprising. The standing rules of the Black Panther Party explicitly stated, "No Party member can join any other armed force than the Black Liberation Army."[16] The BLA underground was composed of independent cells dedicated to the concept of urban warfare. They were active primarily from 1967 to 1973. Their primary goal was to make the United States ungovernable. They believed that armed force was the preferred way to achieve "national liberation" for black people.[17]

A group claiming to be the BLA also distributed leaflets in San Francisco. The flyers threatened drug dealers and prostitutes in an attempt to clean up what the group thought were negative influences in the black community.

New York Panther Assata Shakur became for many the public persona of the BLA. Shakur had been highly critical of the central committee for its suspensions of the New York 21 and other party members. Shakur believed her life was in danger from either Newton or the government during the tense weeks and months of early 1971. She went underground after discovering the government wanted to question her about Panther activities. The government dragnet intensified after a BLA attack on the Manhattan district attorney's house and her picture made the front page of the *New York Daily News*.[19]

Shakur burrowed further into the BLA underground from 1971 to 1973. She believed the members were courageous and intelligent. Still, their inexperience also made them weak and disorganized. Shakur and her friends were compelled to be constantly on the move when their infrastructure proved to be inadequate.[20]

She was captured in May 1973 after a shootout on the New Jersey turnpike. Her friend Zayd Malik Shakur (no relation) and a state trooper were killed during the incident. After a series of trials Assata Shakur was acquitted of all charges for alleged crimes prior to the event on the turnpike. However, she and a colleague, Sundiata Acoli, were convicted of killing the state trooper and were sentenced to life in prison. The BLA engineered her escape from prison on November 2, 1979. Shakur surfaced in Cuba during the 1980s and resides there today despite government attempts to extradite her.[21]

From 1971 to 1973 the BLA was charged with the deaths of eight police officers and one civilian and the wounding of fifteen police officers. Six reputed BLA members were killed in battles with police. Despite these actions the American government was never seriously threatened. Assata Shakur is the only known remnant of the BLA still free today.[22]

The BLA's guerilla warfare, the quarrels in the BPP, and the accompanying political meltdown provoked strong criticism from organizations previously allied with the Panthers. The YLP issued a statement that criticized the lack of democracy within the Panthers and condemned violent acts as divisive and counterproductive.

The YLP also accused the Cleaver faction of overstating the political situation in the United States by claiming that a state of war existed. The YLP maintained that the community did not believe there was any such war, though there was a degree of political repression. The YLP thought it was wrong for either faction to resort to force. Instead, they should seek to outorganize their opponent politically.[23]

The YLP believed that the people would determine which side was correct. "Since the Black Panther Party belonged to the people the people should decide who is to represent their best interests."[24] According to the YLP, only the government would benefit from a war the people had not requested, did not want, and certainly did not need. In the most striking criticism, both factions were accused of mistaking differences with each other for war with the government.[25]

Individuals who were disappointed in the public turmoil also wrote letters to the central committee. They reminded the Panthers that Newton and Cleaver were ultimately responsible to the black community for their actions and urged them to stop the "power play" that was destroying the party and jeopardizing members who were in jail.[26]

The Role of Counterintelligence in the Downfall of the Black Panther Party

Unknown to any party member at the time, a secret government counterintelligence program known by the acronym Cointelpro was actively involved in promoting the downfall of the BPP by fostering feuds within the party and with other organizations.

Cointelpro was not the first government intelligence program aimed at African Americans. During World War I the government had kept a watchful eye on the Industrial Workers of the World, the NAACP, draft resisters, and socialists. The U.S. Army's Military Intelligence Division recruited informers within the black community and subscribed to more than sixty African American publications in its search for information. Government agents such as Major Walter Loving attempted to persuade members of the NAACP and other blacks to temper their criticism of segregation and racism to maintain national unity during World War I. They were very successful in their endeavors.[27]

The FBI began the modern counterintelligence program in 1967 to prevent the rise of a single leader who could unify all the black militant groups. The FBI also said it wanted to stop violence by militants and discredit the groups and their leaders. The government planned to achieve this goal by disrupting, demoralizing, and neutralizing the BPP and other radical groups. It was able to achieve all its goals under the counterintelligence program.[28]

A 1976 United States Senate investigating committee stated that by July 1969, 233 of the 295 so-called Black Nationalist counterintelligence operations were directed at the BPP. These actions ranged from the use of agent provocateurs, wiretaps, and arrests to sending forged letters supposedly written by prominent Panthers to create internal dissension.[29]

One of the most successful government operations against the Panthers was the encouragement of a feud with the US organization in Los Angeles.[30] From 1968 to 1970 the BPP and US were engaged in a bitter fight for power and ideological influence within the black community. The Panther Party believed that a socialist program and interracial alliances based on mutual economic and political interests was the correct path for blacks.

The US organization was the classic cultural nationalist group. It preferred all-black alliances while arguing that Marxism was a white-oriented political philosophy unsuitable for the black community. US accused the BPP of being racial sellouts, and the political atmosphere became very heated.

The FBI sensed a golden opportunity to exploit the disagreements. It sent a series of forged letters, derogatory cartoons, and anonymous death threats to both the BPP and US. The psychological warfare created the mutual impression that each group wanted to attack the other. A series of beatings and shootings culminated in the deaths of the leaders of the Southern California chapter. Jon Huggins, deputy chairman, and Alprentice "Bunchy" Carter, deputy minister of defense, were killed during a dispute over which group would control the UCLA Black Student Union.[31]

The deaths were a tremendous loss because they hindered the BPP's political development and fostered internecine warfare in the black community.[32] The dispute with US troubled relations with other organizations for many years. The Panthers reacted negatively to any manifestations of cultural nationalism no matter how benign.

The FBI was so successful in Los Angeles that it extended its campaign to San Diego and caused similar mayhem. Harassing interviews with party members were conducted, and derogatory cartoons that belittled the BPP and US were distributed in the community. Once again, the idea was to create a confrontation and destroy support for each group.

The US organization shot and killed party members John Savage and Sylvester Bell in San Diego during the summer of 1969. The San Diego headquarters of US was bombed, and one of its members was shot. FBI members assigned to shadow each group kept a tally of the violence and boasted, "That's two for me and one for you guys." A 1969 FBI memo to J. Edgar Hoover also claimed credit for the "high degree of unrest" that occurred from May through August in San Diego. Clearly, the FBI was enjoying its handiwork after setting the conditions for fratricidal warfare.[33]

The bloodshed forced more-moderate organizations in the black community to be more cautious in their relations with the BPP. These groups might have been prepared to form a united front on issues such as prisoners, housing, survival programs, and anti–Vietnam War measures. The political isolation was a direct result of the counterintelligence program.

The government, however, had just gotten started. During the party's 1971 internal crisis, FBI headquarters directed its field offices to "exploit the present chaotic situation within the BPP" by submitting imaginative proposals to encourage the infighting. Cleaver was warned in a forged letter not to send his wife to the United States because of threats on her life. A similar message was sent to Newton's brother, Melvin, warning him of an alleged Cleaver plot against him.[34] Although the Panther leadership had definite differences, it is just as certain that the FBI, through the use of forged letters, rumors, and undercover agents, encouraged and exploited division, mistrust, and violence in the black community and the BPP. Government agents also resorted to anonymous phone calls to local Panther offices, falsely naming certain members as police agents. This tactic led to beatings, paranoia, and, in some cases, people fleeing for their lives. Party morale was undermined further when bureau agents broke up marriages by accusing spouses of being unfaithful to each other.[35]

The FBI also prevented a Panther attempt to enlist the political support of the Blackstone Rangers street gang in Chicago. The FBI utilized its tried-and-true tactics of using agent provocateurs and mailing threatening letters to each organization to provoke an armed confrontation in 1969.[36]

The bureau also "neutralized" the Panthers by attempting to deter individuals from supporting the community programs. Rumors and false letters alleging misconduct and unjust criticism destroyed confidence between Panthers and their supporters. The FBI contacted the employers of Panther supporters and attempted to get them fired.

One letter purportedly written by an outraged member of the public was sent to Union Carbide management and threatened not to purchase stock because an employee was supporting the BPP.[37] There was also a concerted effort to encourage the media to report stories unfavorable to the Panthers.[38]

The Central Intelligence Agency also monitored the activities of the BPP overseas and in the United States. The agency's domestic operations were conducted with the full knowledge that they violated the statutory prohibition on conducting domestic security operations. The CIA's black agents attended funerals, rallies, and other public occasions within the United States in hopes of identifying party members.[39] Agents posing as hotel owners and journalists were also sent to Algeria, Kenya, and Tanzania to monitor Panthers and other black radicals.

The government efforts succeeded because the Panthers were inexperienced in intelligence and counterintelligence matters. The BPP was unable to detect and defeat these elaborate campaigns by well-funded professional intelligence agencies. For example, the FBI developed 7,402 "ghetto informants" between 1967 and 1972. With resources such as these, the counterintelligence program was able to achieve its goal of disrupting, demoralizing, and neutralizing the BPP.[40] The government simply overwhelmed black radicals.

Struggling through the Times: Three Personal Stories

From 1971 to 1974 the BPP was confronted by multiple challenges. Rank-and-file Panthers continued to implement the community programs, responded to a civil war within the party, and worked energetically in Bobby Seale's campaign for mayor of Oakland. They also became aware of the increasing moral and political contradictions of their leaders. Despite these conflicts, each individual Panther continued to work as an activist for as long as he or she could.

These men and women made the community programs function, and they pursued their own vision of social justice despite serious internal and external obstacles. Any understanding of the BPP must include the motivation of the members, why they joined, and what they believed they were working for.

Huey Newton's initiative in beginning police patrols made him the party's natural leader during its early days. The Free Huey movement made him the most famous Panther in the organization by widely publicizing his words and deeds. His early political writings were quoted, constantly reprinted in the Panther newspaper, and bound into pamphlets and widely distributed.[41]

Panthers promoted Newton as the very symbol of revolutionary black manhood, inspiring his adherents to emulate him by picking up the gun. The result was the development of a cult of personality based on Newton's supposed infallibility. The Free Huey movement succeeded in saving him from a murder charge, though he was convicted of manslaughter. A lengthy and ultimately successful appeals process began on his behalf.

Support for the BPP in the black community was controversial, however, because government repression and the constant talk of guns and revolution frightened away many ordinary people who might otherwise have endorsed the Panther stand against police brutality. Some black youth, though, were drawn to the BPP precisely because of its militant advocacy of self-defense.

Moreover, the community programs had great appeal for blacks and whites concerned with social justice. These programs also broadened the party's base of support to a more diverse constituency. One of the most visible signs of that support or curiosity was the party's weekly paper, which sold more than one hundred thousand copies around the world.[42]

Panther recruits were motivated by the belief that the party was a militant organization carrying on the legacies of Malcolm X and black rebellion, wanting to help the black community by participating in the community programs, racial pride, and loyalty to Huey Newton as a charismatic leader. A 1970 Lou Harris poll for *Time* claimed that 64 percent of all blacks surveyed said that the BPP "gave them a sense of pride."[43]

Young urban blacks were often the victims of police misconduct. They were thrilled by the image of armed Panthers facing the police and demanding the right of self-defense against police brutality anywhere in the country.

Joining the BPP was touted in the party newspaper as a natural progression in armed defense of the black community. BPP members claimed they were the latest link in a long line of black rebels that stretched back to Denmark Vesey and Nat Turner. Editorials in the party's newspaper often referred to BPP members as the "heirs of Malcolm."[44]

Other recruits did not necessarily see themselves as warriors. They joined because they believed in the social justice aspects of the community programs. These programs offered individuals an opportunity to address urban poverty. Some Panthers had previous experience as community organizers. They saw the initiatives as an extension of the civil rights movement's call for community empowerment.

Panthers believed their work would raise the consciousness of the black community, educate the people as to the "true nature" of the American political system, and inspire them to work for a change of government.[45] The stories of Eugene Williams, Joe Robertson, and Carol Rucker illustrate why young people joined the Panthers, what they hoped to achieve, and what they actually found as they functioned in the BPP.

Eugene Williams

Eugene Williams (pseudonym) was from the East Coast. Williams's mother and father provided a solid middle-class home for their children, and his childhood was relatively happy. Nevertheless, the family was not unaware of larger social concerns as he grew up. Williams's political journey into the BPP began with his father's death. When Williams was eleven his father had an asthma attack. He died after being denied medical treatment at a so-called white hospital. The death of his father encouraged Williams to become active in church-related civil rights campaigns, and he was present for Dr. Martin Luther King's "I have a dream" speech.[46]

Although he supported King's campaign for social and political equality, he had qualms about nonviolence, believing that every human being had the fundamental right to self-defense. Williams moved to Oakland in 1969. He became interested in the Panthers because of the community programs' social justice aspects and the party's militant reputation for self-defense.[47]

Williams began working with the Panthers after learning of the deaths of Illinois BPP leaders Mark Clark and Fred Hampton. Despite the party's reputation for being a paramilitary organization, Williams, much to his surprise, never received arms training of any kind. His duties included working in the breakfast program for schoolchildren, selling papers, and attending PE classes.

He found there was "a lot of talk" about weapons, but he and his friends had to conduct their own self-defense classes if they wanted to learn. It was not the only contradiction he would become aware of as time went on. Williams had obvious leadership skills, and he was asked to attend the party's ideological institute, where he studied dialectical materialism. He also taught PE classes to high school youth in the community after he became more knowledgeable about party ideology.[48]

Williams worked in Merritt College's black student union in addition to his other responsibilities. The college became widely known as a Panther school because of the large number of party members. By 1970–71, however, the Panther cadre was fairly small (though still influential) because it was extremely difficult to be both a full-time student and a functioning Panther.

Douglas Miranda, a twenty-two-year-old party captain from Boston, was ordered by the central committee to organize the student body. Miranda was a dynamic figure and a gifted organizer who rejuvenated the BPP campus cadre. The cadre organized a breakfast program and PE classes for interested students.

The black students were also embroiled in a dispute with the community college district because the school was moving to the Oakland hills. The students began to call for a strike, demanding the college remain at the same site under community control until a replacement school could be built. In the midst of this turmoil the difference between the living conditions of the rank and file and the party leadership came to Eugene Williams's attention in a dramatic fashion. The discrepancy became a point of increasing tension within the party in the coming months.[49]

Williams's cadre or work group lived out of suitcases in a community center. They slept on mattresses and ate communal meals literally from the same pot. Their income came from selling the party newspaper and from student aid at Merritt College. Most, if not all, of the rank and file had similar communal living arrangements. The severe living conditions did not disturb them because they expected nothing better.

They also assumed that Newton and the central committee had similar quarters. In fact, neither Williams nor most Panthers had any idea where Newton lived. They believed this was because of security concerns, but to their dismay that was not the whole story.

On February 12, 1971, the *San Francisco Examiner* revealed in a front-page article that Huey Newton was living under an assumed name in a $650-a-month penthouse overlooking Oakland's Lake Merritt. The penthouse was furnished with imported furniture. Residents also had access to a doorman, sauna, gymnasium, and a putting green. Newton, David Hilliard, John Seale (Bobby Seale's brother), and Newton's bodyguard had been photographed leaving the building.[50]

Newton was furious and demanded to know how the paper had determined where he lived. The FBI had known about the apartment since November 1970 but had not revealed the location until the Cleaver-Newton schism. The opportunity to create further unrest within the BPP could not be ignored. The contrast between Newton's luxury and Williams's austere conditions could not have been more obvious or painful.[51]

The central committee responded to the public relations problem by claiming that Newton was living in the building because it had much-needed security features. The central committee also maintained that a police attack on the party's leader was unlikely because it would pose an unacceptable risk to his white neighbors.[52]

Community reaction was divided. The BPP received some letters condemning the expensive apartment and pointing out that Newton would be safer in the black community because the police could overcome any alleged security features with little difficulty. On the other hand, a local black newspaper, the *San Francisco Sun Reporter,* supported Newton. It argued that the apartment was well deserved because the party's leader had "put his life on the line." The paper evidently reasoned that the penthouse was a partial reward for Newton.[53]

Reaction within the party was mixed as well. At first Williams and other Panthers attempted to rationalize the contradiction by following the party line. This approach worked momentarily for Williams until events at Merritt College overtook the housing issue. Williams's cadre, under Miranda's leadership, had organized students to protest the impending move to the hills. An extremely successful strike got under way amid widespread community support.

Students believed they had an opportunity to delay the move until flatland residents had an educational alternative.[54]

The administration was on the defensive until opposition to the strike materialized from an unlikely source: Huey Newton. According to Williams, the strike leaders were commanded to shut down their operations because "Newton decided he wanted to be a peacemaker."[55] The reasons for this decision were not entirely clear to the student leaders or Williams. They speculated that the order was designed to increase Newton's prestige and influence with Oakland's black political establishment. In other words, he was enhancing his role as a powerbroker.

The students refused to stop the strike because they believed the orders threatened their educational interests. Williams and his colleagues were in a dilemma. They sympathized with the students because they were aware of the rationale and hard work behind the strike. On the other hand, they were bound by the BPP's orders. Cadre members supported the ten-point program and platform because they believed the ultimate goal of the party was to bring about the exercise of self-determination by the black community.

Williams and his friends defined self-determination to include placing the objective interests of the black community before any other force, personal or organizational. They believed the party should provide an opportunity for the black community to work out its own destiny. Accordingly, Williams's cadre deemed Newton's orders about the strike and his luxury apartment contrary to the interests of the party and the community.[56]

The strike ended under Panther duress. Williams's group went underground to avoid retaliation. Williams was not a part of the BPP underground, but the rules for survival in this netherworld were similar. He managed to stay hidden for a year while more urgent matters occupied the central committee's attention. Newton also encouraged other prominent Panthers to declare their allegiance during the turmoil.

Masai Hewitt (minister of education), Emory Douglas (minister of culture), Elbert "Big Man" Howard (deputy minister of information), and Bobby Rush (deputy minister of defense in the Illinois chapter) signed a public declaration of undying loyalty to Huey Newton and his policies.[57] The declaration was printed in the paper. Miranda's fealty continued to be under suspicion, however, because he was not a Californian. Several East Coast Panthers had publicly criticized Newton's apartment. Miranda "got word that his life was threatened," and he returned to Boston in the spring of 1971.[58] He still faced assault and battery charges in California stemming from the strike and for possessing a false draft card.

Miranda was arrested by the FBI in November and returned to Oakland. He was eventually sentenced to five years' probation for threatening a school of cial. Fortunately, Miranda was able to leave California without any harm after his legal issues were settled.[59]

Joe Robertson

Joe Robertson (pseudonym) joined the BPP at age seventeen. He was spurred by a desire to retaliate for Martin Luther King's death. Robertson's concern about police brutality prevented him from going to Vietnam to "fight someone I did not even know" while police misconduct was occurring at home.[60]

The party was primarily a paramilitary organization for Robertson. He thought the Panthers offered a viable opportunity to engage in guerilla warfare against the government. Robertson had studied Huey Newton's 1967 writings in PE classes. Newton had written that the BPP's aboveground activity would necessarily be short lived before the Panthers had to go underground and conduct military operations.[61]

The Panther underground began in 1967 when Newton named Donald Cox the first field marshal of the BPP because of his alleged attack on San Francisco policemen. The BPP underground grew quickly because of the increasing number of Panthers who were wanted by the police and needed a place to hide. Panthers who were underground were ostensibly under the command of Cox and other field marshals. In reality, attempts at control were unsuccessful, and some of the units were undisciplined.[62]

The security and character of an underground unit was dependent on the mutual trust of the personnel. Going underground meant cutting ties with family and friends. Individuals had to create whole new lives with false identification.[63]

In 1967 Newton had recommended that Panthers study the Russian, Chinese, Cuban, and Algerian revolutions to learn the correct approach to warfare. Guerilla attacks on policemen and the taking of weapons from the government were referred to as "the correct methods of teaching prolonged resistance."

Meanwhile, aboveground Party members were commanded to defend their homes and offices if they were attacked. Anyone who failed to do so risked being expelled from the BPP. As late as January 30, 1971, the party newspaper printed articles on organizing urban guerrilla groups.[65]

These members went underground with the explicit purpose of inspiring the black community to rise up against the government. They believed that the community would assist them because they had convinced themselves that a state of war existed. The possibility that a large majority of the community would not agree that there was a state of war never occurred to them. They also did not consider the possibility that Newton might reevaluate the political situation and change strategies. Any attempt by Newton, no matter how rational, to redirect policy was viewed by the militants as a betrayal of principles and comrades who were risking their lives fighting for self-determination.[66]

The existence of these units was not revealed to many members for security reasons. The opportunity for police infiltration was reduced if a limited number of people knew about their existence. When Williams and his friends went into hiding, it was for their own protection, not for urban warfare. They had to remain hidden because the political situation within the BPP did not allow for principled disagreement.[67]

Joe Robertson and other Panthers had a different outlook. Prior to Newton's change in political direction, Joe Robertson and a significant number of Panthers believed they were mandated by the BPP to prepare for conflict with the government to achieve self-determination for black people. Robertson went underground because he believed the community would support and protect those who were working on its behalf.[68]

Some of these individuals looked to Cleaver as their leader because of his consistent exhortations to armed struggle. His appeal to these members grew after Newton began to retreat from previous Panther positions on urban warfare. Dissidents such as Robertson also knew there was a difference in their material conditions and those of the hierarchy.

Prominent Panthers such as Newton, Seale, and Hilliard had full access to the organization's funds while ordinary members found it difficult to have adequate food, clothing, or shelter. Michael Tabor, a New York Panther, charged that money raised for party use while Newton was on a 1971 East Coast speaking tour went to him personally. Tabor accused the party hierarchy of living a luxurious lifestyle while local branches and chapters "were starving to death."[69]

Individuals who attempted to question the allocation of funds were treated as disloyal and expelled. The BPP thus disappointed many otherwise loyal members by not providing the structure for principled criticism. The dissidents began to style themselves as the "real Black Panther Party" and started to publish their own newspaper replete with criticisms of the central committee for reactionary politics and corruption.[70]

It was inevitable that bloodshed would occur in such a volatile atmosphere among armed adversaries with charges and countercharges being hurled. On March 9, 1971, unidentified assailants killed prominent dissident Robert Webb on 125th Street in Harlem. The breakaway faction promptly charged that Newton had ordered the assassination. Sam Napier, the circulation manager of the BPP newspaper and a Newton loyalist, was murdered on April 17, 1971, in New York. His death was widely viewed as retaliation for the slaying of Robert Webb.[71]

These killings sobered some partisans on both sides. Joe Robertson and others questioned how the black community benefited from the loss of two men who were widely known and highly respected within the party. Neither Williams nor Robertson believed that using guns was the way to resolve differences with former comrades. They saw the dispute as spiraling out of control with no adequate solution in sight for either of them.[72]

Williams and Robertson lived in the underground's shadow world for two and ten years, respectively. Williams surfaced when he was arrested for an unrelated matter. Robertson came in from the cold in 1980. It had become apparent to Robertson that the black community had made a choice that did not involve the use of arms to achieve what were essentially political goals. His idea of revolution was over before it started.[73]

Carol Rucker

Carol Rucker was nineteen when she joined the BPP in San Francisco. She served from 1969 to 1974. Rucker supported the party as an organization dedicated to ending police misconduct and achieving "freedom" for the black community. She had followed the civil rights movement prior to becoming a Panther and had some political knowledge. Dr. King's death deeply affected her as it had many other BPP members. She also believed there was an unequal distribution of political and economic resources in her community. She thought the party's programs could address the problem.[74]

Rucker attended PE classes, participated in physical training, and worked in distribution for the newspaper. Party recruits in the San Francisco branch, like other Panthers, read Marxist literature. Still, the ten-point program and platform was the best ideological explanation for Rucker and many others. Rucker was also willing to cede a great deal of personal autonomy to the party in order for the collective to function as a disciplined unit.

Rucker was articulate and intelligent, and increased responsibilities came her way. Unlike Williams, Rucker remained in the BPP during the split. Eventually she was placed in charge of securing donations from San Francisco businesspeople. Rucker's position allowed her to observe how the leadership handled funds. She made the same discovery as Michael Tabor. All of the money collected was not going back into the programs. A substantial portion was being siphoned off for personal use by the leadership.

The misappropriation was the subject of community rumors. The result was that being a Panther was no longer something that community residents routinely honored and respected. This was especially difficult for Rucker because the party had become a large part of her personal identification. She believed that although the programs were worth saving, there was only so much one person could do. She resigned despite not being able to bring all her previous ideals to fruition. Though Rucker's resignation did not lead her to open rebellion, like the New York Panthers, the ethical issue was obviously as personally disturbing to her.[75]

The Effect of the Split on the General Rank and File

Party life was a strenuous experience emotionally and physically. The rank and file began work early in the morning and continued until late at night. Members worked in the survival programs and on the newspaper. They had to attend PE classes and organize door-to-door in the community. In addition, there was the very real threat of being arrested or injured by the police. The Panthers claimed the loss of twenty-eight members to police brutality or government-inspired plots between 1968 and 1973.[76]

Outside observers disputed that claim and reduced the number killed by the police to ten. Furthermore, they challenged the innocence of the Panthers in each instance.[77] In any case, the most salient fact is that some Panthers died and many others were incarcerated. Organizational and personal survival was aided under these conditions by establishing group cohesion. Panther cadres lived in communal settings, worked as a team in the community, and faced common dangers and problems.

Physical danger was so common that Panthers worked out a system of non-verbal distress signals to be used when necessary. Hand gestures and other signals alerted other members to situations such as "shady characters with hands in pockets," time to leave, or a desire to talk quietly with other Panthers.[78]

Members also achieved a feeling of accomplishment and satisfaction through the successful functioning of community programs. The ten-point program became a reality for them through the shared experience of working in medical clinics, liberation schools, breakfast programs for schoolchildren, and community organizing. Participation in the movement solidified their feelings of self-determination and liberation and enhanced their group solidarity.

But group solidarity broke down when Panthers resolved disciplinary issues with physical violence. This type of discipline was called "mud-holing." It referred to a beating administered by other Panthers. Former Party leaders David Hilliard and Elaine Brown have acknowledged that members accused of violating organizational rules were subjected to corporal punishment.[79]

The potential for miscarriages of "justice" and the misuse of power are obvious. Abuse by the police was a fact of life for Panthers. Abuse by their friends was traumatic and unexpected and eroded the loyalty of the rank and file. It added to the emotional and physical toll of party life and contributed to the attrition rate. It also made the escalation of violence against other Panthers easier.

The deaths of Webb and Napier were made easier because of the previous use of force to resolve disagreements within the organization. Principled dissent, simple mistakes, or misinterpretations were equated with disloyalty or being an agent provocateur. This atmosphere made it easier to label loyal members as so-called enemies of the people.

The existence and toleration of physical abuse, ethical violations, a cult of personality, and a lack of inner-party democracy were the result of political inexperience. They also resulted from some leaders' lust for power. Many members were willing to tolerate shortcomings because they believed they were in a war with the government. They thought that any attempt to deal openly with these problems could weaken the group at a critical moment. Unscrupulous individuals capitalized on this reluctance.

When internal contradictions or government pressure became too much for some members, they simply stopped reporting for duty and dropped out of sight. Eventually, former members attempted to "live a normal life again," but if they had a police record, that might take years to achieve.[80]

In any event, some were dogged by a sense of having let down their friends who remained behind. Those who remained were willing to wait and see whether their patience and loyalty were to be rewarded. These were the men and women ultimately responsible for implementing "survival pending revolution."

5

WOMEN AND THE BLACK PANTHER PARTY

It is our belief that the role of Black Women is the same as everyone else in the struggle to educate, mobilize, organize, and fight to the best of her ability. The word revolutionary has no gender. It is neither masculine or feminine. It is neutral, which means a revolutionary can either be male or female.

—*Right On!,* December 1971

From 1971 to 1980 the Black Panther Party tried to change its public persona from being revolutionaries to being a political reform organization. Women stepped to the fore at this time and led many of the survival programs. This was fortuitous for the party because the reputations of their top male leaders had been severely damaged by political killings and revelations of financial turpitude. The new political direction would have to be productive to wipe out the memory of recent disasters.

The decision to turn away from arms to community service aided women's rise to prominence within the BPP. The slightly higher educational level of women prepared them for key positions in the organization's schools and medical clinics. The BPP conducted a skill survey of 119 members in 1973. The fifty-two women and sixty-seven men were from throughout the nation.

Forty-two women (81 percent) had graduated from high school, and thirty-three (63 percent) had at least one semester of college. One woman had a bachelor of science degree. Forty-six men (68 percent) had graduated from high school, and twenty-nine men (43 percent) had at least one semester of college. One man had a bachelor of arts degree. The surveys revealed that men and women performed the same jobs within the party's ministries of health, information, and culture. Men and women also worked as secretaries with the central committee, in the finance cadre, and in the area of legal defense.[1] The story of the women's struggle for equality is an integral part of the history of the BPP.

From Tarika Lewis, generally acknowledged as the first woman to join the Panther Party, to JoNina Abron, the last editor of the newspaper, women worked diligently to further the organization's goals. They also had to wage an ongoing battle to change male perceptions of their proper role within the BPP.

The decision-making and leadership roles of women in the Panther Party increased exponentially from its founding in 1966. At the same time, however, there was a wide range of personal and ideological experiences within the BPP. As a result, there was no all-encompassing male or female experience during the party's existence.

The first indications of a changed role for female Panthers occurred in 1969 when the government killed, incarcerated, or drove into exile many of the male leaders. Government repression forced the Panther Party to forsake artificial gender categories and use personnel in the most logical manner. At the same time, female members, aware of their ability, began to demand that they be treated as comrades-in-arms, not merely clerks or sexual partners. The organizational changes required a great deal of adjustment on the part of men. The reality that women were taking the same risks facilitated the process.

Political change over time and a constant influx of recruits also meant that there was never a static party attitude on women's liberation. In addition, the position of women cannot be considered separately because men were influenced by similar social factors, though their reaction may have been different. The struggle for respect and equality took place throughout the party's existence.

Even though the gender equity issue sometimes damaged internal relations, it never overshadowed the Panthers' dominant political message of community empowerment. Panthers were thus more or less inclined to accept changes in gender status depending on their individual makeup, the time period they served in the BPP, the nature of the change, and the caliber of local and national leadership.

In many ways the Panther Party mirrored the larger society's attempts to solve the "woman question." The American people, buffeted by a decade of political unrest, war, and cultural change, struggled to redefine themselves in the 1960s and the early 1970s. Many women, regardless of race or income status, were restive and dissatisfied with their traditional role in society.

They sought a more active place outside of their traditional family duties. A far-reaching social movement, inspired by the civil rights struggle, sprang up, seeking more female participation and influence in politics, business, academia, and labor.

A feminist political community also sought to compensate for what its members saw as years of exclusion from the power and participation to which they believed their numbers and skills entitled them. The BPP became part of this struggle when female Panthers fought to secure what they believed was their rightful place in the struggle: side by side with men.

Early Panther Philosophy

The Panther Party was founded during a period of intense Black Nationalism. Early recruitment efforts were influenced by a strong male-dominated blend of politics and social theory. Cultural nationalists in particular articulated a male-centered worldview. The Nation of Islam, Ron Karenga, and Leroi Jones (Amiri Baraka) were particularly well known. Cultural nationalists argued that women should be relegated to a mystical position as "mothers of the nation," subordinate to men in all areas except child rearing.

This philosophy bore many similarities to the confining pedestal of so-called respect and honor allegedly occupied by white women. The nationalist pedestal was similar in the fact that it was more apparent in myth than in reality. The nationalist philosophy was steeped in patriarchy because men defined the category and the rationale for it. The most common rationale was the "protection" argument.

The advocates of this argument believed that female sexuality and public conduct needed to be controlled for the good of the community. One rationale for this position was that black women had been subjected to sexual abuse during slavery and its aftermath. This argument was extremely appealing to some men on a psychological level. Blacks were aware that the larger society's dominant ethos called for men to protect women's honor from abuse. Black men were also painfully aware that this had not always been possible in the past. This humiliating knowledge grated both on them and on women.

Consequently, the emotional appeal was obvious when some nationalists called for men to step forward and assume traditional protective and leadership functions. Both men and women could agree on this issue. Nevertheless, there were two problems with the argument.

In the first place, it seemed to blame women for male behavior. In other words, a woman's mere physical presence could be a distraction or enticement to many men. Some nationalists advocated a type of sexual segregation to eliminate such issues. The Nation of Islam was held forth as a model, with their all-male Fruit of Islam and female Muslim Girls Training organizations. Each of these groups socialized men and women to their "true" social role in family and public life.

The second problem arose with the demand that women step back from most, if not all, decision-making roles in the civil rights movement. Many women and some men could not see the justice or logic in what they viewed as a discriminatory and self-defeating tactic. Why, they asked, should the movement be deprived of one-half its brainpower and energy? Where was the concept of equal rights?

These were entirely proper questions, and the nationalists tried to answer them with varying degrees of success. When they were pressed, cultural nationalists would grudgingly concede gender equality for the sake of political harmony. They preferred to argue, however, that men and women were not so much equal but complementary. In other words, each sex had important though different and biologically determined roles. Modesty, thrift, and service were to be the special concern and province of black women. Deference to men in general and strict obedience to husbands was encouraged.[2]

For example, Elaine Brown relates a story about a social event in Los Angeles where women served the food. Women, however, were told not to eat until the men were finished. The rules were made and enforced by the US organization with Ron Karenga present.[3]

Another common idea was that women should voluntarily restrain any impulses to compete with black men for fear of undercutting male authority and thereby damaging the masculine psyche. This belief was allegedly rooted in a desire to bolster black men, who historically had been oppressed and prevented from fulfilling their true role as heads of the family.

Huey Newton had argued in one of his earliest essays that the lower-class black male had been deprived of his masculinity because a racist society regarded him as an inferior human being. Newton maintained that the black male's lack of education and employment skills prevented him from providing for his family. Consequently, his wife was prone to regard him as worthless because of his inability to satisfy society's basic definition of masculinity. In addition, Newton claimed that the wife was probably the main breadwinner of the family because white men did not perceive her as a physical threat. In other early writings, Newton contended that men could begin to fulfill their protective duty to black women and children by joining the BPP's warrior society.

It is not known how much of this argument reflected Newton's own fear and doubt. Elaine Brown claims that Newton had a poor formal education and read very slowly. Brown also says that Newton "wrote" his books with the aid of a tape recorder. At any rate, his masculinity argument was quickly accepted in the BPP.[5]

Eldridge Cleaver's book *Soul on Ice* contributed to patriarchal practices within the BPP by engaging in a provocative psychosexual discussion of American society. Cleaver argued that America regarded black men as supermasculine menials and black women as amazons who had been alienated from their feminine nature. Cleaver's theory also posited white women as hyperfeminine sex objects and white men as the intellectual but physically weak controllers of the planet.

Cleaver maintained that in addition to political warfare, white and black men were engaged in a battle for sexual access to and control of each other women. The victor would control society, and the women's role was to be a passive prize for the successful combatant.[6] *Soul on Ice* was a national bestseller and a runaway hit in the BPP. Many Panthers read the book and internalized Cleaver's pronouncements about sexual politics.

Some party women articulated a deferential position during 1967 and 1968 in the *Black Panther*. They assumed that the female role should be, among other things, a helpmate and a constant encouragement to men, as opposed to an equal and assertive partner. Panther Judy Hart argued that "the first and foremost stimulus is and will be the black man. Women are magnetically attracted to men and black men are, in 1967, the only men on the scene. Women cannot help but gravitate toward life—and the black man holds within the strength and the fiery passion of his struggle, his life, the life of his people and his posterity. His total commitment to his life is an invitation to the black woman to join with him in the pursuit of a life together."[7]

A female Panther who identified herself as a "Black Revolutionary" wrote: "The Black woman should take a supportive roll [sic] in bringing about the awakening of the black consciousness of her man. Her main objective should be to assist in the re-birth of the black man's mind. Her part is by no means small. She should let him test this new mind; let him feel secure in this new consciousness. In this way he can grow as his mind expands.... It is a woman's duty to find the beauty in life and to unfold this beauty before the eyes of her man and children."[8]

Linda Greene wrote later that same month that women should try to be "everything" to a man and seek out his needs to fulfill them. Gloria Bartholomew urged women to stand behind and beside black men (symbolizing simultaneous deference and support) in their common fight for liberation.[9]

These writers advocated that the black woman should be a type of superwoman: a feminine fighter who would not emasculate her man with criticism and questions. In other words the black woman was asked to rise above human nature and not question any errors that men made.

These arguments ultimately failed because the Panthers discovered through their own experience that restricting women to subordinate roles was impractical for several reasons. The dominant zeitgeist of the 1960s was toward political empowerment for those who had historically been outsiders. Black women were certainly oppressed outsiders. It would have been politically inconsistent and foolish for the Panthers to relegate a large portion of their membership to an inferior status. Furthermore, the BPP's ideological models in Cuba, China, and Vietnam advocated complete equality for women.

Whether this was the actual social reality in these countries is another question. These governments publicly decreed that women should not be bound by outdated cultural conventions that restricted them from reaching their full human potential. More important than foreign influences, however, were the words of Malcolm X, who also argued that only backward societies prevented women from fulfilling their human potential.

The recent work of such civil rights activists as Ella Baker, Diane Nash, Fannie Lou Hamer, and Victoria Gray was certainly known to a man as knowledgeable as Malcolm. He understood that he had to shed his earlier NOI-inspired beliefs in female subordination if he wanted to be accepted by many women as a true secular leader on the national stage. Consequently, Malcolm began to contend that those who claimed to want progress must provide incentive for women to participate, or they virtually enshrined underdevelopment.[10]

Last and most important, the Panthers had their own experience to consider as they discovered women were fully capable of exercising leadership. The participation of women in the most crucial events of party history was key to enhancing their position in the BPP.

The Change in the Role for Women

Twenty-four men and six women were present at the 1967 Sacramento demonstration that protested a proposed gun control law. One of the women was a University of California-Berkeley law student, Barbara Auther. Auther gave a sidewalk press conference and claimed that the BPP was armed only for self-defense against police brutality. She denied that the Panthers had broken any laws but also doubted whether the demonstration would convince any assemblymen to vote against the proposed legislation. Auther was right. The Mulford Act passed overwhelmingly.[11]

The six women were apparently not full-fledged members because Panthers generally acknowledge that Tarika Lewis became their first female member in 1968. Lewis (known then as Matilaba or Joan Lewis) became politically active in high school when she and other students founded a black student union.

The BPP appealed to Lewis because the group wanted to end police brutality. Lewis was an excellent artist, and her community murals and drawings in the *Black Panther* were instrumental in publicizing the party's early political message during the Free Huey movement. Lewis's artwork transcended gender roles, but throughout 1968 other women were usually assigned to clerical and other traditional functions.[12]

For instance, during her first visit to Oakland in 1968, Elaine Brown was routinely assigned to food preparation and kitchen cleanup for communal meals. According to Brown, other women resented her indignation because they believed she was trying to rise above her (their) station. Female Panthers had their own officers during the Free Huey movement in 1968, and they also reported to a national captain for women. This position was abolished during the 1968–69 reorganization, and after that time, personnel began to be assigned to jobs solely on the basis of qualifications.[13]

The party's most well-known woman on the national level during 1968 was the communications secretary, Kathleen Neal Cleaver. Kathleen Cleaver had left college to become an SNCC worker. She and her husband, Eldridge Cleaver, were the only married couple on the central committee. Bobby and Artie Seale were married, but Artie was a secretary at national headquarters.

Kathleen Cleaver's and Lewis's positions and influence, however, could be regarded as individual achievements until Ericka Huggins changed the overall position of Panther women. Huggins was the first woman to lead a party chapter. The office also began a liberation school and breakfast program. In 1969 Ericka Huggins, Jeannie Wilson, Francis Carter, Rose Smith, Loretta Luckes, Peggy Hudgins, Maude Francis, and seven men, including Bobby Seale, were arrested and charged with murdering a fellow Panther, Alex Rackley, who was suspected of being a police informer. This group became known as the New Haven 14.

Huggins and the six women were the BPP's first female political prisoners. Their cases were instrumental in changing party thinking on gender roles. Francis Carter, Rose Smith, and Maude Francis were pregnant at the time of their arrests, and two of the women gave birth while in detention.

Female Panthers reasoned that if they were risking their lives and going to jail, then it was time for them to assume or be assigned more responsibility. Their claims were bolstered because the continuing police offensive against the BPP demanded a rational use of all members. The BPP was faced with a choice: Black Nationalist patriarchy or the progressive trend advocated by Malcolm X. The choice was clear. The repressive actions of the U.S. government and an evolving ideology combined to encourage the BPP to redefine women's role in the party.

Eldridge Cleaver's public change is particularly noteworthy. The *Black Panther* published a long letter from Cleaver to Huggins in 1969. The letter praised the courage and commitment of Panther women. It also called on men to drop all manifestations of chauvinist behavior and regard women as equal partners in the struggle. In addition, women were encouraged to do "whatever they want" to avoid being relegated to an inferior position.[14] This was a far cry indeed from the man who had admitted to raping black and white women in his prior career as a street criminal.

The role played by women in New York and Los Angeles during 1969 also represented the winds of change within the BPP. Joan Bird and Afeni Shakur had joined the New York City chapter in 1968 and were part of those swept up during the mass arrests following the alleged New York 21 bomb plot. Shakur was promoted to section leader because arrests had decimated the chapter leadership. Bird was badly beaten during her arrest in New York. In addition, six women were wounded during the December 1969 police attack on the Los Angeles office.

In 1968 the *Black Panther* had printed articles about Panther women unfolding beauty before the eyes of men. By 1969 it was obvious that the BPP was far beyond that cultural construct. Beauty was of no use during police attacks or lengthy incarcerations. Membership in the BPP and belief in its ideals had earned Panther women the rough equality of being shot at and incarcerated like their male colleagues.[15]

Safiya Bukhari epitomized the transition from appendage to comrade. Bukhari was in the BPP and the BLA from 1969 to 1983 and served almost nine years in prison for bank robbery. Bukhari was a seventeen-year-old college student in 1969 when she first encountered the BPP in New York. She was arrested because she intervened when a policeman arrested a Panther for selling newspapers.[16]

Her experience with the police and the jails influenced her to join the BPP. Bukhari's duties were as varied as other Panthers. She worked in liberation schools and the breakfast program as well as sold papers and taught PE classes. She also performed welfare rights organizing. Her community organizing "beat" was from 116th Street to 125th Street in Harlem.[17]

Political prisoners were a major focus of BPP organizing. The Panthers constantly had major trials throughout the country. Bukhari worked on the New York 21 case. As a result, she was subpoenaed by the grand jury in 1973 to get information against other Panthers. She was offered immunity from prosecution to persuade her to testify, but she decided to plead the Fifth. Her decision meant she was liable to receive five years' imprisonment for refusing to testify.

She made the decision to go underground and join the BLA. Bukhari remained free until her 1975 arrest in Norfolk, Virginia, for bank robbery. It was common for BLA members to stage what they called "expropriations" to strike against the state and obtain survival money. Bukhari was convicted and sentenced to twenty-five years but managed to escape in December 1976 before being recaptured in February 1977.

She was incarcerated for eight years and eight months before being released in 1983. While incarcerated she and other inmates started a group called Mothers Inside Loving Kids (MILK). The group's purpose was to help convicts safeguard parental rights by being able to spend time with their children. Bukhari was released in 1983 and journeyed to Cuba to spend time with former BLA member Assata Shakur. Bukhari's story illustrates the speed with which some women were converted to the revolutionary cause as well as the depth of their commitment. Safiya Bukhari died August 24, 2003, after a long illness.[18]

Panther women publicly articulated the party's position on gender discrimination in 1969 when Roberta Alexander spoke at the United Front against Fascism Conference in Oakland. Alexander acknowledged that there was an ongoing struggle in the Panther Party against sexism and male chauvinism. She claimed that it was being handled in the "correct way" through political education and that women were "more and more taking on a leadership role" in the organization.[19]

At the same time, however, Panther women resisted being part of what they regarded as the white-dominated women's liberation movement. The BPP also published a dialogue with several female members in 1969. The interview was widely circulated in leftist political circles because the Panthers styled themselves as the vanguard of the American struggle. Consequently, there was a great deal of interest in whether the Panthers would assign primacy of place to women's issues. If they did not, how would they justify the omission to erstwhile colleagues on the Left?

The female Panthers argued that in the party's worldview men and women were not enemies. They were partners working together to solve a mutual problem of oppression, and there should be no artificial political separation between them. They maintained that any separation was incorrect because "that's an example of how the women's struggle is taken out of perspective—it is separated from class struggle in this country, it's separated from national liberation struggles and it's given its own category of women against men. To the extent that women's organizations don't address themselves to the class struggle or to national liberation struggles they are not really furthering the women's liberation movement."[20]

They went on to stress that their lack of identification with the mainstream women's liberation movement did not translate into a willingness to tolerate male chauvinism in the BPP. They also said chauvinism could be either a male or female problem because it was defined as an unreasoning love for one's own gender. The women also contended that Panther men had to learn that their manhood did not depend on subordinating black women.[21] This issue was an ongoing battle because some men thought that any increase in female authority meant a concomitant diminution in their masculinity.

Panther women did not consider themselves feminists in the same mold as the National Organization for Women because they did not believe the struggle was based on gender differences. The Panthers believed that many white women wanted to integrate into the existing system to reap its bene Panthers, on the other hand, would have said they wanted a completely new society, with drastic changes in the political and economic structure.

The BPP wanted to defeat capitalism and racism. They argued that sexism was only a reflection of women's unequal racial and economic position and that it should be opposed within a larger context. Therefore, gender equity could only be a subset or a manifestation of deeper changes. In other words, Panthers believed they had multiple targets in their sights whereas the National Organization for Women had only one. These core beliefs reigned supreme despite the party's internal problems between men and women.

The University of California's Graduate Assembly held a conference in 1990 on the legacy of the Black Panther Party. One of the panels featured Belva Butcher, Kiilu Nyasha, Sheba Haven, Tarika Lewis, Majeeda Rahman, and Artie McMillan, who discussed their party experiences.

Belva Butcher and Kiilu Nyasha assumed positions of authority and responsibility within the BPP in 1969 and 1970. Butcher was eighteen years old when she joined the BPP in 1968 to oppose police brutality. Butcher organized PE classes in Oakland housing projects before being promoted to field secretary and sent to Connecticut to build political support for the New Haven 14. She became an assistant to the central committee while on the East Coast and worked with Robert Webb on planning the RPCC. Butcher also worked in the Philadelphia chapter's liberation schools and lead abatement programs. She left the BPP during the 1971 schism after becoming disillusioned with the central committee's financial and political practices.

Kiilu Nyasha was a legal secretary and antipoverty worker in New Haven before becoming breakfast program coordinator with the Panthers. Nyasha also worked on the New Haven 14's defense committee in 1970–71. Majeeda Rahman joined the BPP in 1970 and founded the first Intercommunal Institute after Huey Newton directed her to take charge of educating the children of party members. Rahman continued to work with Panther children until 1972, when she left the party.

Artie McMillan described her journey from an inexperienced and somewhat naïve young woman to becoming the first secretary of national headquarters. McMillan believed that although female voices were not initially heard in the Panther Party, women, through hard work, eventually brought their own strength to the organization.

These and many other women exemplified the changes the party went through from 1966 to 1971, when female Panthers began to believe and demand that they should be treated with the respect to which their work entitled them.[22]

Living through the Change in Roles: Individual Experiences

The careers of Lu Hudson and JoNina Abron underscore the intricacies of the Panther experience. Lu Hudson was a politically conscious twenty-year-old when she began searching for an organization interested in social change. The Panther Party's ten-point program and platform appealed to her because it demanded the same political rights and protection for blacks that were guaranteed for white Americans. The deaths of Fred Hampton and Mark Clark helped to persuade her to join the BPP because the Panthers were risking their lives to institute relevant social programs. Hudson began functioning as a community worker in 1969 with the Baltimore BPP.[23]

The Baltimore chapter ordered its recruits to sell newspapers, work in the breakfast program, and attend weekly PE classes before becoming full-fledged members. Hudson also worked with Charles Garry on the New Haven 14 case before eventually being transferred to Oakland in 1972, where she worked in voter registration for the Seale-Brown campaign and at the Intercommunal Institute. Hudson displayed an avocation for legal work in Oakland, and she spent most of her Panther career in the legal services programs.[24]

Hudson believed the BPP's social programs were an example of what the community could do on a larger scale if properly organized. Still, she had felt increasingly isolated after Elaine Brown's 1977 departure because Brown had served as a buffer between her and the party's male chauvinists.[25] Hudson resigned from the BPP in 1979 after a series of personal disputes. Some of the problems centered on her plans to go to law school. Another woman resented her "individual" goals because law school would reduce the time she could reasonably spend on party affairs.[26]

Despite the circumstances of her resignation, Hudson credited the party with "giving a sense of pride and direction for those not willing to be spit upon and beaten without defending themselves. It provided training and skills for some people who would have been considered among the dregs of American society. It also eventually encouraged a pragmatic approach to change as evidenced by the proliferation of former BPP members on college and university campuses as students and instructors today. The social programs were a much-needed Band-Aid for the black community and an example of what could be done by the community itself."[27]

She also learned management and other organizational skills in the BPP. Hudson believed, however, that the day-to-day work done by the rank and was never fully appreciated by many in the party's leadership. As a result, " lack of appreciation for the rank and file led to the abuses of power and corruption that frequently accompany a rise to power by those who had not previously exercised authority."[28]

JoNina Abron served in the BPP from 1972 to 1981. Abron was a twenty-four-year-old college graduate with a master of arts degree in journalism when she joined the Detroit branch in 1972. She transferred to California in 1974 and worked on a variety of projects before becoming the last editor of the *Black Panther* in 1978.[29]

Abron was pleased to join an organization that, she thought, believed in the equality of men and women. Her subsequent experience, however, showed that the Panthers, like other men and women, still had to struggle against "backward" ideas. Abron wrote a memo to Newton in 1977 protesting the discriminatory treatment and male chauvinism she had encountered within the party. For example, she was upset with the ban on women having relationships outside of the BPP.[30]

The ostensible reason given was that men could recruit women into the organization, but no "worthy" man would allow himself to follow a woman into the party. Despite this stricture, some women, with the support of female Panthers, did relate to men outside the party. Abron believed there were women who could maintain principled relationships with men who, though not necessarily potential Panthers, were still making a contribution to the community. Abron argued that women should be given the same freedom as men in their personal life, and she urged the creation of a panel to give direction to men and women who chose to have relationships outside the party.[31]

Abron also maintained that women in the party were only respected if they were leaders because ideas from rank-and-file women were rejected, whereas the same idea from a female leader would be accepted. She attributed this to the overall low status of women, though she admitted that some women also had the same attitude toward men who were not leaders. Abron urged Newton to rid the BPP of chauvinists and closed her memo by declaring that she expected more from her comrades precisely because they were party members and should be setting the example for society.[32]

A female Panther named Dale also complained to Newton about her male colleagues: "We Black Panther women who don't like to go out...or who are suppose to be available for those late night runs can become lost. The abuse and misuse of women by the males in the party has almost totally discouraged me. Within past months a comrade slopped into bed with me and began to disrobe me and have sex, to which I firmly objected and he did finally give up." Dale did not mention any investigation or punishment, and there is no record of a response by Newton to the problems of women such as Dale.[33]

In fact, sexual relations and family life within the BPP were complex matters. For instance, Lu Hudson recalled that "it was difficult to convince men to abstain or have protected sex to avoid spreading venereal diseases or other infections among the women."[34] Although some men were progressing beyond these actions, their social practice was on a continuum, with some being further along than their comrades were.

The issue was further complicated because at that time there was a widespread belief in the black community that birth control was a genocidal plot to limit population growth among people of color.[35] This idea resulted in some women not practicing birth control.

Audrea Jones, a party leader from Boston, attempted to address the problem in 1972 by proposing a family planning policy. Her proposal included standardizing postnatal recuperation periods and joint decision making on pregnancies. Men and women would decide to have a child and submit their decision to a review process, which would determine whether the timing was compatible with the party's political and material needs. Jones's suggestion was never implemented, but her proposal was a unique approach to an overwhelming organizational problem.[36] Jones's effort, however, was not the end of bureaucratic "solutions" to the Panther population explosion.

In 1974 Newton ordered all Panthers to practice birth control for two years. The directive obviously failed because babies continued to be born. There is no record of anyone being punished for violating the order.[37] In any event, Panther women, like those in the larger society, continued to bear major responsibility for birth control.

As the party grew, many people joined who were either already parents or began families while in the organization. Party leadership had never imagined the BPP would become responsible for caring for so many children. They were temporarily at a loss as to the right approach. Communal child care performed by Panthers was one response to the problem. This was less than satisfactory for some members.

Tommye Williams wrote to Newton and expressed her sorrow and frustration with not being able to spend more time with her son than "Sundays when there is no meeting and several hours each evening three nights a week." requested more time and stated she would leave if a solution were not found for her individual situation. Williams maintained that the collective should not be given sole authority to raise children because children needed to spend time with their biological parents. She contended that each child matured at an individual rate and that parents should monitor their children's exposure to academics and sports. Williams asserted that children and parents were too often almost strangers to each other.[38]

Party life and family duties often conflicted with each other. Sometimes Panthers chose traditional family concepts over a political obligation. They left the BPP because they could not reconcile family life with the rigors of membership. Other women were somehow able to combine both obligations. In any event, these intensely personal issues were difficult to resolve.[39]

Sexual Relationships

Intimate relations extended from traditional marriages to "Panther weddings and nonexclusive sexual relationships. Young, unmarried female Panthers were encouraged to have sexual relationships only with members who were deemed sufficiently revolutionary. This practice was allegedly intended to encourage male militancy.[40]

Panther weddings were nonclerical ceremonies where the couple exchanged revolutionary vows of commitment to the struggle and each other. Four of these weddings were featured in the *Black Panther* during 1969. Charles Bursey and Shelley Sanders participated in the party's first "revolutionary wedding" on May 1, 1969, at St. Augustine's Episcopal Church in Oakland. Bobby Seale officiated at the ceremony and read *Quotations from Chairman Mao*.[41]

The Kansas City chapter quickly followed with another ceremony on May 16, 1969. Pete O'Neal, the deputy chairman, united Phyllis Story and Phillip Ortega in "revolutionary marriage." O'Neal also used the "little red book." An honor guard displayed shotguns and sang revolutionary songs to entertain guests.[42]

Traditional ministers also performed church ceremonies for some members. Father Earl Neal performed the marriage services for Black Panther minister of culture Emory Douglas and Judy Graham at St. Augustine's Episcopal Church. Neal read standard verses from the Bible and quoted a passage from *Soul on Ice* titled "To all black women from all black men."[43]

The Reverend Dick York married minister of education Ray "Masai" Hewitt and Shirley Neely at the Berkeley Free Church on August 19, 1969. The *Black Panther* noted that the ceremony was traditional, "with some parts altered and most of the metaphysics removed." Presumably some of the altered parts referred to were the wedding rings. The North Vietnamese government donated the rings. They were allegedly made from a U.S. plane shot down over Vietnam. The pilot's fate was not mentioned.[44]

Although the weddings united two people, sexual fidelity was an individual decision. In fact, people who were married in traditional ceremonies prior to joining the BPP were not necessarily in monogamous relationships either. This was because multipartner relationships were common in the BPP. Participants in multipartner relationships were purported to be an example of revolutionary detachment from traditional relationships and free from bourgeois emotional attachments. This goal was not always achieved.

Elaine Brown, for example, admitted she was jealous of Huey Newton's wife and his other partners. Brown herself was the victim of one of her other lover's jealous rage. David Hilliard's open marriage was satisfactory to him until his wife also engaged in a sexual affair with Newton. Hilliard was eventually accused of violating some newly promulgated rules on sexual behavior before his incarceration, and he was expelled while in prison.[45]

Many Panthers attempted to function in these liaisons. In almost every instance, however, the result was less than satisfying to one or both partners. This was only one level of frustration, because lower-ranking male and female members also had the unpleasant experience of having their partners commandeered or seduced by those in higher positions.

Sequential polygamy and the abuse of power could and did invoke feelings of jealousy, anger, and fear. The BPP found out, like others before them, that there were unforeseen difficulties and consequences inherent in any radical departure from traditional norms of marriage, family, and sexual exclusivity.

Causes for the Change in Roles

Like other contemporary American organizations, the Panthers confronted gender equity issues throughout the 1960s and 1970s. The struggle within the party was made more intense by political radicalism. The Panthers were attempting to build a new society, and the party was their vehicle for doing so. Female members expected their organization to be on the cutting edge of social change. They were bitterly disappointed when male chauvinism and traditional gender roles proved to be more resilient than expected. At the same time, however, female Panthers were full of revolutionary fervor. They were confident that changes in gender relations would eventually occur.

Men dominated the organization from 1966 through 1968. This had to be changed for several reasons. First, the government's anti-Panther offensive was constantly incarcerating many of the male leaders on the national and regional levels. Second, the party's ideology and rhetoric were espousing liberation for all oppressed people. Presumably this included gender equity for women. Third, women began insisting on equal treatment in response to the revolutionary rhetoric and changed circumstances. In other words, both internal and external factors forced a more active role for women in the BPP. Opportunities existed for the actual participation of women at all levels of party activity. Increased authority in turn bolstered self-confidence and altered the female role within the organization.

The numerous rank-and-file women were the real harbingers of change.

They played a major role through their tireless work around the country. These women gave their minds and bodies to the struggle. Female Panthers internalized slogans on self-determination, liberty, and respect. They believed that their male comrades would support them through equal treatment. In reality, they would insist on their political rights while still being subjected to varying degrees of sexual harassment.

Women had to struggle against being reduced to marginal positions either by the larger society or within the party. The success of their efforts rested all too often on men's ability to be receptive to change. The willingness and ability of men to treat women on an equal basis, however, was a constant struggle.

Assata Shakur, among others, has written about how difficult it was for men to be friends with a woman without having any sexual agenda. Shakur credits her friend and colleague, Zayd Shakur, with treating women with respect and refusing to participate in any sexual harassment. Not surprisingly, these actions were only part of Zayd Shakur's political qualities. He was also described as being an excellent organizer with a high degree of patience and understanding. In other words, Zayd Shakur's willingness to participate in new gender relationships was enhanced by his progress in other social areas.[46]

Many personal relationships within the BPP also tended to disadvantage women and encourage their sexual exploitation. Interestingly, the effort to redefine sexual relationships was billed as a progressive attempt to free men and women from allegedly outmoded sexual practices. But the attempt to encourage free-floating sexual unions, allegedly with no emotional attachments, was ill advised. It did not take historical or personal experience into account. Not surprisingly, men and women found it difficult to deviate from traditional social practices.

They continued to have deeply engrained personal feelings of sexual exclusivity and jealously. In addition, some men no doubt had multiple partners and exploited their female colleagues under the guise of being progressive.[47]

Many young women probably would never have had the opportunity to exercise any political power or responsibility at all if it had not been for the Panthers. Certainly, it is doubtful that the opportunity would have occurred so early in their lives. JoNina Abron, Audrea Jones, Lu Hudson, Majeeda Rahman, and Belva Butcher, among others, exercised major administrative and leadership functions as Panthers.

Women achieved positions of trust and responsibility because they fought for them. Women also consistently demanded respect while pointing out contradictions between rhetoric and practice.

The contributions and struggles of party women should not be overlooked, because male chauvinism and sexual harassment were not completely defeated. This has not yet occurred within the larger society. The Panthers, however, deserve credit for the areas where they did make progress. The lack of total success does not diminish their effort.

6

DECLINE AND FALL

It was arrogant of us to imagine that we were going to save the people. It is the people who will save themselves. If any kind of vanguard movement like the Panthers should point up the contradictions in the system...they do it through newspaper articles or through the conventional process not through violent acts.

—Huey Newton, August 1980

As a reform organization the Panthers argued for the black community to receive its fair share of the conventional political pie. The reform mission included an intensely fought 1973 Oakland mayoral election, increased interaction in mainstream political affairs, and a surprising involvement with the spiritual community. The vast majority of members believed in these missions, and they worked diligently to carry them out. Nevertheless, the bright beginning of the Oakland election campaign was also the beginning of a series of devastating scandals that also engulfed the survival programs.

An older and decreasing membership was forced to confront the reality that the community no longer found them relevant. Other, more attractive political options existed. Government welfare efforts dwarfed the financially strapped survival programs of the party. The Black Panther Party had come into existence, flourished for a while, and then went out of existence. The community took note of its work and moved on.

The reform effort began with the dismissal of murder charges against Seale and Huggins in New Haven. They returned to California in May 1971 to rejoin the BPP. Newton placed Seale in charge of the survival programs, and soon thereafter Seale coordinated a rally where one thousand bags of groceries and four hundred pairs of shoes were given away. The party pressed ahead with these activities, and ten thousand bags of groceries were given away in March 1972 during a three-day Black Community Survival Conference in Oakland. Contributions by community businesspeople and proceeds from sales of the newspaper picked up the cost of the event.[1]

The Panthers wanted to turn the survival programs into a government-sponsored initiative as a demonstration of their power and the viability of the new political direction. They needed to be in political office to achieve this goal. In May 1972 Bobby Seale and the new minister of information, Elaine Brown, announced that they were going to run for mayor of Oakland and city council, respectively.[2]

It was not the first time that Panthers had run for elective office. Eldridge Cleaver had run for president in 1968 on the Peace and Freedom Party ticket along with Huey Newton for Congress and Seale and Kathleen Cleaver for the California State Assembly.[3]

This time the emphasis was different. The 1968 campaigns were widely understood to have been a consciousness-raising effort. The Panthers intended to win in 1973. Electoral politics were a logical step because victory would be seen as justification for the 1971 political transition.

Newton believed that the Panthers had to reorganize themselves in order to run a credible campaign. That meant a major shift in national resources to Oakland. The attempt to win political power in Oakland translated into a simultaneous diminution of local resources nationwide. Many local chapters and branches were closed to move members to Oakland for the campaign. Some Panthers resisted this move because they were reluctant to leave communities where successful local programs existed. In addition, they had comrades in jail who needed their support. The resisters left the BPP, taking their discontent with them.[4]

The leader of the Illinois chapter, Bobby Rush, was a notable exception. Rush supported the central committee and believed that electoral politics marked a return to the party's original vision of community service.[5]

The members who were shifted to Oakland exhausted themselves going door-to-door registering voters, passing out campaign literature, and staging rallies. The results were impressive. By the last week of March they had registered thirty-five thousand new voters. This boosted the black proportion of the electorate in Oakland to 50 percent of the overall total.[6]

The Panthers also began reaching out to the black middle class after years of criticizing them for mindless materialism. Seale acknowledged that the BPP needed to provide a framework in which the black middle class could work.[7] But it was a limited concept because he was only encouraging them to donate their time to the community programs, not be a part of the decision-making process. Power sharing or political input apparently was not on the agenda.

Seale's campaign platform was based on advocating increased community service and the use of the power of government to eliminate unemployment. Seale and Brown planned to increase revenue by taxing stocks and bonds, increasing capital gains taxes, and raising the rental on the Oakland Coliseum. The money from this revenue would in turn be used to hire social workers, rehabilitate housing, and improve infrastructure throughout the city.[8]

Seale and Brown expected to win the minority-dominated flatland community. They believed the mainstream candidates would split the remaining vote. They campaigned in the Latino community by endorsing bilingual ballots for local elections. The party appealed to the gay community by advocating a ban on housing and job discrimination as well as an end to police harassment. They also pledged themselves to work for an end to antigay discrimination in adoption, child custody, taxation, inheritance, and prisons. These initiatives foreshadowed later political efforts by several years.[9]

The Panthers were full of confidence after Seale forced a runoff with the incumbent mayor. Sixty-three percent of the electorate voted in the primary. Mayor Reading finished first, with 55,434 votes, which was eighty-four votes short of avoiding a runoff. Seale was second, with 21,329 votes. Brown lost her race 55,811 to 34,866, even though she received more votes than Seale. Seale expected to receive all of Brown's votes in the runoff. Coretta Scott King, the Reverend Jesse Jackson, the American Federation of Teachers, and Assemblyman Willie Brown endorsed Seale in the general election.[10]

Interest was high in the general election, with 70.9 percent of the electorate voting. Seale lost, however, 77,634 to 43,749. He blamed the loss on fifty thousand of his presumed supporters failing to turn up at the polls even though they were registered. Apparently, not voting was too much of a habit for new registrants to overcome regardless of the candidate.[11]

Nevertheless, Seale and the Panthers had demonstrated the possibility that a well-organized campaign by the Left could defeat the political establishment. Following the election the BPP attempted to reach out in other political directions as well. The central committee debated whether Bobby Seale should be allowed to join the Urban League and the NAACP but was unable to reach a decision before Seale left the party in 1974.[12]

Chicago's Bobby Rush was allowed to attend the Black Political Convention in Arkansas. The convention's goal was to create a national black political agenda for what the attendees believed were African American interests on the national and local levels. They hoped the agenda would be independent of both major parties. African American organizations were supposed to carry out voter registration drives, conduct voter education programs, and endorse candidates for office.[13]

The central committee, in a burst of caution, prevented Rush from committing the party to any actions. In any case, no long-lasting independent political initiatives ever came out of the convention, and the initiative died.

The outcome of the election, however, resulted in more Panthers returning to their homes around the country. Their disillusionment was the result of more than an election loss. It was also a reaction to the leadership's apparently uncontrollable propensity for unethical behavior. This propensity caused problems for the rank and file and threatened to disrupt their political efforts.

Misdeeds and Their Effects

Newton and his inner circle were involved in several violent incidents from 1972 to 1974. Drug use among the leadership became flagrant and was to blame for many of the episodes.[14] Each incident served to bring the Panthers into further disrepute, and one was particularly egregious. In 1972 local papers reported that Fritz Pointer, a sociology instructor at Oakland's North Peralta Community College, the flatland successor to Merritt College, was attacked and beaten in his classroom by several Panthers.[15]

Pointer had engaged for some time in a wide-ranging philosophical discussion of Panther policies. Party leadership apparently believed that Pointer was attacking the Panthers. During one of these discussions, several unidenti assailants burst into the class, kept the students and a security guard outside, and beat the instructor. The security guard initially identified the attackers as bodyguards for Bobby Seale.[16]

Seale was reported to be on the East Coast at the time of the beating. Almost immediately after the incident, Pointer began to deny that the party was involved. He claimed the beating was a "personal thing" and had not been done at the direction of the Panthers.[17]

The BPP took the position that the accusations were part of a slanderous attempt to embarrass them and prevent Bobby Seale from becoming the mayor of Oakland. Pointer and the BPP, however, were not strangers to each other. In 1967 the instructor had been a member of a rival organization that styled itself the Northern California Chapter of the Black Panther Party. Hilliard, Seale, and Newton derided the group as "Paper Panthers" because they were not militant enough. They were ordered to cease using the Panther name, and they complied. There was only one BPP after that.[18]

Pointer did not press any charges for the beating. It was not clear why. It was clear, however, that despite the reform image, serious problems remained with the Panther reality.

Many party members became disillusioned when the community registered disapproval of the BPP's negative activities. Negative publicity regarding violence and financial misdeeds had a detrimental effect on the public despite the community programs. The rank and file, Sisyphus-like, pushed the community programs uphill against the misdeeds. The central committee, on the other hand, seemed determined to push the party downhill through self-destructive behavior.

The year 1974 proved to be another period of crisis for the BPP. Several of the party's leaders were either purged or forced to resign. Elaine Brown claims these expulsions were the result of Huey Newton's drug-induced paranoia. David Hilliard and his brother were expelled for violating BPP rules. At the time of his expulsion, Hilliard was serving a prison sentence for his role in the Bobby Hutton shootout. Chairman Bobby Seale and his brother were also forced out for disloyalty. Newton himself was involved in several unsavory incidents during 1974: a barroom brawl with undercover police officers, the assault of a tailor, and the accusation of murdering Kathleen Smith, a teenage prostitute. Newton would flee the country for Cuba after the murder accusation. He would remain there until his return in 1977 to finally face the charges.[19]

The rank and file might be forgiven a sigh of relief after the departure of their leaders. They might also have wondered whether those leaders had left too late to do any good. The Black Panther Party would continue, but it would undergo substantial policy and personnel changes. It had to regroup once again in an effort to recoup its prospects after suffering from a string of scandals.

Elaine Brown assumed the chairmanship and led the party until Newton return in 1977. She and the Panthers would try to repair their tattered image during the interim through involvement in city politics and government boards and commissions, especially those relating to BPP educational programs.[20]

Ericka Huggins, director of the BPP's Community Learning Center, became a member of the Alameda County Board of Education in 1976 when she ran unopposed in her district. Huggins and Mayor Lionel Wilson served on the board of directors of the Educational Opportunities Corporation, the parent organization of the Community Learning Center, from 1975 to 1977.[21]

Audrea Jones was elected to the Berkeley Community Development Council. Jones also led the George Jackson Free Health Clinic in Berkeley after Sheba Haven left the BPP in 1971. In addition, Panther women ran for antipoverty offices in Chicago.[22]

Brown again lost in her bid for city council in 1975, but she was more successful in getting out the vote for other politicians. Panthers were used as campaign workers in the election of Alameda County Supervisor John George and Mayor Lionel Wilson. Both men were the first blacks to occupy their respective offices. Brown was also a California delegate to the 1976 Democratic convention and became a behind-the-scenes power broker when the Panthers began working with mainstream political organizations.

Reconnecting with the Church

The BPP also tried to reconnect with that venerable institution, the black church. The BPP had an up-and-down relationship with the black church throughout its history. Many ministers had allowed their churches to be used for events in 1968 during the Free Huey movement. Later, during a burst of so-called revolutionary enthusiasm, David Hilliard accused the church of being involved in oppressing blacks.[23]

These attacks displayed political immaturity and a lack of historical knowledge by the Panthers. The BPP leadership evidently did not know or care that the black church was born out of a need to enable African Americans to survive slavery. During slavery many white Americans saw Christianity as a vehicle for social control and emphasized St. Paul's dictum that slaves should obey their masters.[24]

Many Panthers were aware of Nat Turner and Denmark Vesey as slave rebels but were completely unfamiliar with their Christian background. At any rate, the BPP stopped many of its attacks in 1969. This was entirely in its self-interest because churches possessed ideal facilities to have liberation schools and breakfast programs for schoolchildren.

In fact, the first Panther breakfast program was established at St. Augustine's Episcopal Church in Oakland. The church's pastor, Father Earl Neal, was a veteran of civil rights work in Mississippi. He had been a spiritual advisor to Huey Newton during his 1968 murder trial.[25]

Father Neal encouraged other ministers to allow their churches to be used for community survival programs. Neal also urged the creation of a resource bank of church members so that the community could utilize the talents of these people. The BPP also worked with the Reverend Charles Koen, a community activist from the Cairo, Illinois, United Front, who preached a sermon on behalf of Panther prisoners in New Haven, Connecticut.

Other politically involved ministers had also united with local chapters around issues of mutual interest. They believed the church was intertwined with the survival and well-being of black people.[26]

The BPP took the ultimate step in 1973 when it founded the Son of Man Temple as an interdenominational church in Oakland. The Panthers intended the temple to be an example of how a church should be involved in the community. The temple was a nondenominational place of worship. Nevertheless, it also sponsored all of the party's survival programs and served as a community forum for lecturers. Organizers from African liberation movements and W. E. B. DuBois' stepson spoke at the temple.[27]

The Son of Man Temple was an attempt to reconnect with a community institution that had the respect of large numbers of people. The party had finally recognized that ideology did not necessarily prohibit spirituality and politics from mutually beneficial cooperation.

The BPP eventually managed to establish a working relationship with black ministers after several rocky years. The Panthers had curtailed their politically immature criticism of the church. They began to relate to ministers as men who could possibly serve a valuable function within the survival programs. Furthermore, before Huey Newton went into exile, he acknowledged that during the 1966 to 1971 era the Panthers had been wrong to attack the churches so vociferously and offered to work with them to benefit the community. Finally, in 1973, members began working to improve their knowledge of the black church by having written quizzes in PE classes.[28]

The Main Contradiction

It seemed that the Panthers were on the road to recovery when they became reacquainted with violence and scandal in the familiar person of Huey P. Newton. Newton returned to Oakland in 1977 to stand trial on charges of murdering a prostitute and assaulting a tailor. He began to reassert control over the party and organized all operations around his trial. The results were disastrous.

An unsuccessful attempt to kill a key prosecution witness occurred the evening before Newton was scheduled for a preliminary hearing in his murder trial. Two Panthers died as a result of this incident, and several others were arrested.[29] Subsequent investigations revealed that the BPP's Oakland Community School employed the arrested Panthers.[30] The negative publicity regarding the school and a series of embarrassing audits prompted the mayor's resignation from the board of directors. Elaine Brown resigned from the BPP, citing health reasons.

Huey Newton's murder and assault charges were dismissed later when juries were unable to reach a verdict. His legal troubles, however, were far from over. He was found guilty in 1978 and 1979 of being an ex-felon in possession of a gun and was sentenced to prison in 1981 after a lengthy appeals process.

Not even the famed survival programs were exempt from unethical behavior. Newton also received a six-month jail term in 1988 for embezzling a $15,000 state education check intended for the Panther community school. He had originally been accused of embezzling $600,000 and charged with thirty-three counts of grand theft. All but one count was dropped as part of a plea bargain.[31]

Newton's conduct embarrassed and demoralized the members and played a major factor in the party's declining reputation. The BPP was reduced to fi eight members by 1979. There were only twenty-seven in 1980. In addition, most Panthers were between thirty to forty years of age, and one-third were more than thirty-five years of age.[32]

This was a far cry from 1967 to 1973, when the vast majority of members were in their teens and early twenties. The only functioning party operations were the Oakland Community School, a print shop, and Huey Newton's legal problems. Some Panthers obtained part-time jobs to sustain themselves, but full-time party work was still expected. It was no longer possible physically or emotionally for Panthers to be completely dedicated to their work. Community support was also lacking.[33]

A 1979 memo to Newton frankly addressed what was called "internal deterioration" in an attempt to halt the inevitable death of the party. Several reasons were given for the obvious decline: the elitist attitude of the leadership in directing people's lives through threats and regimentation, the lack of an independent and stable economic base for political activities, and the absence of any professional development for the members. The cadre was "technically and intellectually backward," and every attempt to address the situation was blocked by the central body to preserve its own power.[34]

Suggestions for change included calling for an emergency party congress with the power to call for a vote of confidence or no confidence and the ability to elect a new central committee. The recommendations were not acted on, and the malaise continued until the inevitable end occurred.

The spirit that prevailed in the nation during the Reagan presidency was completely different from the 1960s. Realistically, there was no political victory in sight for the BPP. As a result, party morale was lower. The remaining members left because there was no point in going on. In addition, they were concerned about their own economic and personal futures. External attacks and internal mismanagement had combined to cause the death of the Black Panther Party.

EPILOGUE

All of us who saw our leaders murdered, our people shot down in cold blood, felt a need, a desire to fight back. One of the hardest lessons we had to learn is that revolutionary struggle is scientific rather than emotional. . . . Decisions can't be based on love or anger. They have to be based on the objective conditions and on what is the rational, unemotional thing to do.

—Assata Shakur, 1987

The Black Panther Party has a legacy of activism, courage, commitment, miscalculation, and missed opportunities. These young men and women exhibited an extraordinarily high level of personal and group dedication to their vision of social change. Week after week, headlines in the *Black Panther* informed readers that Panthers were being shot, beaten, bombed, arrested, and investigated throughout the country.[1]

Panthers demonstrated commitment and courage because they believed in their mission. The BPP was an outlet for many black youth looking for a positive direction in their lives. They did not expect to achieve financial or other material gain; in fact, many anticipated a hard life, and they were not disappointed. Panthers organized the African American community by demanding an end to police brutality, establishing survival programs, calling for a constitutional convention, and running candidates for political office.

Nevertheless, the lack of clarity concerning goals and methods, the absence of democracy, and the inability to prevent innergroup violence kept the organization from fulfilling its promise as a progressive political party. Courage is not enough to defeat your enemies. Clarity of goals and methods is essential. Panther influence was at its height when blacks identified with the political message of self-determination and community development.

Conversely, Panther fortunes declined when the leadership became divided, politically confused, and no longer able to portray the BPP convincingly as an advocate of social change. The party's decline also occurred when affirmative action began to open up more opportunities in employment and education. Police attacks, scandals, and internal disarray also inhibited potential recruits.

Panthers thought the civil rights movement was too passive in emphasizing the nonviolent attainment of voting rights and equal access to public accommodations. Panthers argued that blacks were also concerned with police brutality, jobs, and housing. Consequently, the BPP recruited members who took an aggressive approach to these issues.

Nevertheless, these concerns did not originate with the Panthers. Dr. Martin Luther King's support of the Memphis sanitation worker's strike and his Poor People's Campaign show that he understood the importance of economics. Stokely Carmichael also had written about the need for blacks to be more involved in economic matters.[2]

The government was never in danger from the BPP's or anyone else's military activity. There was, however, legitimate apprehension about what the Panthers might accomplish politically. The attempt to reach across racial and economic lines could conceivably have been the spark for a far-reaching reform movement, especially in a time of widespread social and political unrest. The political approach was especially successful when after an initial emphasis on military struggle the Panthers began to espouse a more pragmatic approach to change, as evidenced by the survival programs, the Intercommunal Institute, and the Seale-Brown election campaign.

The BPP did not achieve "national liberation," but they inspired numerous activists and community members to make greater efforts toward self-help and political involvement. The survival programs and the party's call for blacks to be more proactive in controlling their own affairs were a continuation of the civil rights movement's efforts to empower the black poor.

The focus on police brutality eventually led, in many cities, to the establishment of civilian review boards that investigated instances of police shootings and other misconduct. Breakfast programs and medical clinics pressured government agencies to increase their community outreach to counter party efforts. These and other programs around the country epitomize the Panther drive for community empowerment.

The party's existence became problematic, however, when government poverty programs surpassed BPP efforts. The *Black Panther* ceased publication in 1980. The Huey P. Newton Educational Institute closed its doors in 1982 after graduating its last class. There was no need for an official announcement. The third era was over, and the BPP was history.

From 1966 to 1982 the BPP claimed to be the vanguard of a new American Revolution primarily because of its acknowledged losses in confrontations with the government. This is understandable because few contemporary civil rights groups sacrificed as much for their beliefs.[3]

Panthers also believed their survival programs and revolutionary commitment inspired the community to exercise self-determination, and the rank and file as well as program participants achieved a sense of liberation by working for it under difficult circumstances. One has to question, however, whether there was another way to accomplish the goal of community empowerment without the death and incarceration of so many young people.

There is no doubt that Newton's confrontational tactics during the party infancy were bold and daring and that they drew thousands of recruits. It is also just as clear that the tactics were essentially ad hoc because neither Newton nor Seale had a comprehensive ideology at that time.

Furthermore, the tactics were based on an uncritical acceptance of Robert Williams's and Malcolm X's nascent self-defense message. The assassination of Malcolm X in 1965 made him a martyr, and his ideas became virtually unassailable for many young militants. This was unfortunate because Malcolm's ideas had still not been fully developed. They were accepted, however, as if they were the result of long contemplation and practice.

Malcolm was under tremendous pressure during the last sixteen months of his life. He traveled overseas twice, made numerous speeches, and tried to develop a coherent political theory that would be a foundation for his fledgling national organization. It would be up to his admirers to test his political theories in the cauldron of actual practice. Many of the young militants forgot one of Malcolm's dictums: never be afraid to expand your knowledge, question your own beliefs, and change them if they are proven wrong.[4]

Too many black radicals believed this concept applied only to the civil rights movement's integrationist philosophy and nonviolent tactics. They were wrong because critical thinking also applied to the whole concept of armed struggle in the pursuit of independence. Most blacks were not pacifists, but they were divided on the use of force. How and when was it to be applied? What was the purpose? This division increased when force was discussed in relation to nationalism. It was difficult for nationalists even to define their goals.

Did they want reform or revolution? What was the definition of each? How was the goal to be achieved? What was the purpose of using arms? Robert Williams's career could have been instructive.

Williams originally adopted his self-defense strategy as an *adjunct* to nonviolent protest. His original intent was to discourage Ku Klux Klan violence against unarmed protestors asking for their constitutional rights. Williams was driven into exile because the state had superior military resources. He became more militant during his eight-year exile. His newspaper, the *Crusader,* urged blacks to ally with the world's anti-American forces. The Republic of New Africa and the Revolutionary Action Movement elevated him to official positions within their organizations. Williams, however, wanted to return home, and he did. His actions after his return were instructive.

Williams resigned his positions in the Republic of New Africa and the Revolutionary Action Movement. He lived quietly and made no revolutionary pronouncements. In fact, he criticized the BPP and other black radicals for not having a coherent strategy. He believed many groups were too dogmatic and isolated from potential allies. Williams also critiqued the lack of military expertise of those who claimed to be willing to use violence. Privately he said that he had always believed in the Constitution but that the government did not respect the document when it allowed the mistreatment of its citizens.[5]

In fact, full acceptance as American citizens had been the main thrust of the black struggle since the first emancipation of slaves after the Revolution. This particular historical lesson was forgotten or ignored by many black radicals (including Williams during his exile) because it did not fit into their worldview. In addition, the whole idea of using arms might only be viable if it was acknowledged to be temporary and directed against vigilantes and extralegal force.

In that way it would be a bargaining chip influencing the government to fulfill its duty of protecting black citizens from vigilantes or police brutality. In any event, it would certainly be a problematic option. Malcolm never had the opportunity to define clearly the exact purpose of using arms. Perhaps, for his own reasons, he was not inclined to do so. Many blacks might agree to the limited use of self-defense to protect themselves from such depredations as the 1963 bombing of the Sixteenth Street Church in Birmingham or the beatings and assassinations of civil rights workers.

Guerilla warfare to achieve autonomy from the U.S. government, however, was not realistic to most blacks. Furthermore, urban riots were not a precursor to revolution despite the radicals' wish to interpret them as such. Instead, they were outbreaks of political frustration, usually with an immediate cause: police brutality.

In fact, the Panthers were initially involved with arms only because they wanted to stop police brutality. Patrolling the police, however, as Newton himself acknowledged, could only be a short-term tactic. If it was going to be done at all, it should have been accompanied from the beginning by a political goal of establishing community review boards to monitor police brutality.

The BPP, however, did not begin to talk about using the political system to institute community control of police until 1969.[6] Years later, Newton claimed that picking up the gun was only a temporary organizing tactic, but neither his fellow Panthers nor community people understood it that way, and it was not articulated as such at the time. The lack of clarity in goals and methods was detrimental because the early military strategy severely limited the party's immediate political options. The government took the BPP at its word—"off the pig"—and treated the members as guerillas. Robert Williams saw clearly that despite their revolutionary rhetoric the overwhelming majority of Panthers never had any kind of comprehensive military or counterintelligence training.

Consequently, most of the membership was completely unprepared psychologically and materially for the government's Cointelpro operations. Nevertheless, the rank and file carried on. The human losses were so severe, however, that by 1971 the BPP leadership had publicly disavowed the idea of immediate armed struggle. Survival (of the organization) pending revolution became the first order of business.

The question naturally arises: if the policy was correct in 1971, then why not in 1968? The failure to implement this policy earlier led to the death of many young people who had placed their faith in the leadership.

From 1968 through 1971, however, there was a disagreement in the leadership about whether the group could win a showdown with the government. The party's left wing thought that African Americans, other minorities, and young whites could achieve self-determination through force of arms.

On the basis of their later actions, presumably Newton and Seale believed otherwise. They were incarcerated, however, and could not easily change policy. Furthermore, most of their support was dependent on maintaining a revolutionary image. Any retreat while in prison could be interpreted as a collapse under pressure. This would certainly alienate their allies and most of the membership. In addition, no other central committee member had the stature, authority, or conviction to advocate a policy change.

The members of the rank and file were conflicted. They supported the survival programs but had never completely withdrawn from the concept of armed struggle. In addition, whenever offices were attacked, as they were from 1968 through 1971, members were forced to defend themselves or be killed. It was suicidal to abandon self-defense. They were in an ideological dilemma. Did they want reform or revolution? How was either to be achieved?

Joe Robertson, Eugene Williams, and Assata Shakur maintain that Panther political education efforts were too reliant on Frantz Fanon's justifications for revolutionary violence, dialectical materialism, and Mao Zedong's writings.[7] The central committee's inability to develop a workable, understandable, and comprehensive progressive ideology grounded in the *American* experience was a serious error. The overwhelming majority of the black community never felt comfortable with or understood the Marxist philosophy promulgated by the BPP because it was outside of their experience. Panthers themselves had problems with it.

Maurice Cornforth's book on dialectical materialism was required reading at the BPP ideological institute, but his philosophical ruminations on quantitative and qualitative change were never fully understood by most members.[8]

The party succeeded whenever it focused on solving concrete day-to-day problems, that is, police brutality, food, schools, and health care. It fell short in the ideological arena because its members were speaking a language that the majority of American people, black and white, did not understand or appreciate.

The BPP could have served as an independent force in local, state, and national elections, capable of being an honest broker for African American interests and fulfilling one of Malcolm's goals—an independent political party that could not be controlled by the two major parties. It could have been a party that held the balance of power in tightly contested local and national political races. The emphasis on arms was the major (but not the only) reason that promise was not achieved.

Last, there is the ethical issue. Political leaders should demonstrate openness and accountability within their organizations. This is especially crucial when lives are at stake. Leaders must be held to a high standard of accountability. Lack of accountability breeds secrecy and disdain for members and the community.

The BPP membership was tolerant to a fault. Their forbearance did not serve them well. Political dogmatism and secrecy were the rule. Financial matters were concealed from the membership until 1979. There is no excuse for this state of affairs, whether it occurs in the NAACP, the BPP, or any other political organization.

Americans should make an intense study of the Panther experience. Democracy, responsibility, and openness must prevail in community organizations. Secrecy to avoid public embarrassment must be prevented. There must be clarity of goals and methods. Rank-and-file members were the heart and soul of the BPP. Huey Newton and Bobby Seale founded the organization, but all generals must have troops. The rank and file believed they could make a difference by working to improve their communities and thereby demonstrating their capacity for self-determination. These men and women believed they could achieve "national liberation" in America.

They were not victorious, but the United States is still sprinkled with activists who learned their organizing skills in the Panther Party. They work in medicine, sociology, prison advocacy, life-skills counseling, the law, sports psychology, the arts, academia, and politics. Most former Panthers (like other survivors of the sixties) acquired skills, got married, raised families, and explored other ways to serve the people.

The rank and file's courage and dedication resulted from youthful idealism and a devotion to the principle of self-determination. Panthers wanted to prove that African American people were capable of reclaiming their dignity and that they could accomplish whatever they set out to do. A relatively small band of young men and women established themselves throughout America and attempted to provide for the defense and social welfare of their communities. They did a difficult job under hazardous circumstances for as long as possible.

The African American community also agreed with the concept of self-determination. Most of them, however, believed that goal could be achieved nonviolently within the American political system. The BPP eventually saw the wisdom of this decision. Those who once wanted to lead now realized they had to follow. The people will only be led where they want to go. The Black Panther Party learned this fundamental lesson at a tremendous cost. It should not go unheeded.

NOTES

Introduction

The epigraph to this section is from Huey Newton, speech delivered at Boston College, November 18, 1970, in Huey P. Newton, *To Die for the People: The Writings of Huey P. Newton,* ed. Franz Schurman (New York: Random House, 1972), 31.

1. Charles William Hopkins, "The Deradicalization of the Black Panther Party: 1966–1973" (Ph.D. diss., University of North Carolina at Chapel Hill, 1978); Kathleen Cleaver, "The Evolution of the International Section of the Black Panther Party in Algiers, 1969–1972" (senior essay, Yale University, 9 December 1983); Kit Kim Holder, "The History of the Black Panther Party, 1966–1972" (Ph.D. diss., University of Massachusetts, 1990); Angela Darlean Brown, "Servants of the People: A History of Women in the Black Panther Party" (senior honors thesis, Harvard University, 1992); Tracye A. Matthews, "No One Ever Asks What a Man's Role in the Revolution Is: Gender and Sexual Politics in the Black Panther Party, 1966–1971" (Ph.D. diss., University of Michigan, 1998); Robyn C. Spencer, "Repression Breeds Resistance: The Rise and Fall of the Black Panther Party in Oakland, California, 1966–1982" (Ph.D. diss., Columbia University, 2001); Paul Alkebulan, "The Role of Ideology in the Growth, Establishment, and Decline of the Black Panther Party: 1966 to 1982" (Ph.D. diss., University of California-Berkeley, 2003).

2. U.S. House of Representatives, Committee on Internal Security, *Gun-Barrel Politics: The Black Panther Party, 1966–1971,* 92nd Cong., 1st sess. (Washington, D.C.: Government Printing Office, 1971), 69–80.

3. Diahhne Jenkins, "Socialism: Serving the People," *Black Panther*, 1 November 1969, 19; "Illinois Chapter Free Medical Clinic," *Black Panther*, 18 October 1969, 3.

4. Eldridge Cleaver, "On the Ideology of the Black Panther Party," *Black Panther*, 6 June 1970, 12–15; New York 21, "Open Letter to the Weather Underground," *East Village Other*, 2 February 1971, 3.

5. Memo, FBI director to all offices, on Counter-Intelligence Program, Black Nationalist Hate Groups, Internal Security, 25 August 1967; FBI memo, G. C. Moore to W. C. Sullivan, on Counter-Intelligence Program, Black Nationalist Hate Groups, Racial Intelligence, 14 May 1970, *The Counter-Intelligence Program of the FBI* (Wilmington, Del.: Scholarly Resources, 1978), 30 reels.

6. Huey Newton, "On the Defection of Eldridge Cleaver from the Black Panther Party and the Defection of the Black Panther Party from the Black Community," *Black Panther Intercommunal News Service,* 17 April 1971, suppl., C–F.

7. Ollie A. Johnson III, "Explaining the Demise of the Black Panther Party: The Role of Internal Factors," in *The Black Panther Party Reconsidered,* ed. Charles E. Jones, 403–6 (Baltimore: Black Classic Press, 1998).

8. Ibid., 406, 407.

9. Pearl Stewart, "Black Panther Party Falters," *Oakland Tribune,* 27 November 1977, 2C; George Williamson, "Police Tell Theory of Black Panther 'Purge,'" *San Francisco Chronicle* 8 December 1977, 1; Abron Papers, Black Panther Party Archives, Howard University, Moorland-Spingarn Research Center, Washington, D.C.

10. Elaine Brown, *A Taste of Power: A Black Woman's Story* (New York: Pantheon, 1992), 437–50.

Prologue

The epigraph to this section is from Huey P. Newton, "A Functional Definition of Politics," *Black Panther,* 17 February 1970, 3.

1. Mary L. Dudziak, *Cold War Civil Rights: Race and the Image of American Democracy* (Princeton, N.J.: Princeton University Press, 2000), 3–17.

2. W. E. B. DuBois, *Dusk of Dawn: An Essay toward an Autobiography of a Race Concept* (New York: Harcourt, Brace and Co., 1940), 192–204.

3. Ibid., 200.

4. Stokely Carmichael and Charles V. Hamilton, *Black Power: The Politics of Liberation in America* (New York: Vintage Books, 1967), 46, 47, 58–84.

5. Elijah Muhammad, *Message to the Blackman in America* (Chicago: Nation of Islam, 1965), 161–64. The Muslim program of "What We Want, What We believe" strongly infl enced the Black Panther Party's 1966 ten-point program and platform, especially in regard to political autonomy. The party revised the Nation of Islam's point number 10 and called for a UN-supervised plebiscite to determine the national destiny of black people. The call for a plebiscite was deleted in 1972 and replaced with a phrase calling for control of modern technology. The reason for the change will be discussed in the first chapter.

6. Bobby Seale, *Seize the Time: The Story of the Black Panther Party and Huey P. Newton*

(New York: Vintage Books, 1970), 4–12; David Hilliard and Donald Weise, eds., *The Huey P. Newton Reader* (New York: Seven Stories Press, 2002), 23–43.

7. Malcolm X, *Ballots or Bullets*, audio recording of speech made April 3, 1964 (Detroit: First Amendment Records, 1964). This speech was made after Malcolm's expulsion from the NOI and prior to his trips to Mecca and West Africa. Malcolm discusses politics, Black Nationalism, the internationalization of the civil rights struggle, and guerilla warfare.

8. Hilliard and Weise, *Huey P. Newton Reader*, 49.

9. Ibid., 45–49.

10. Seale, *Seize the Time*, 85–99; "Let Us Organize to Defend Ourselves," *Black Panther*, 25 April 1967, 2.

11. Black Panther Party, "What We Want What We Believe," October 1966 platform and program, *Black Panther*, 7 June 1969, 21.

12. "State Police Halt Armed Negro Band," *Sacramento Bee*, 2 May 1967, 1; Don Ferrell, "Black Panthers Believe Arming Is Needed to Fight 'White Oppression,'" *Sacramento Bee*, 3 May 1967, A-12; "Black Panthers Are Arraigned in Case Involving Capital Invasion," *Sacramento Bee*, 4 May 1967, 1.

13. Central Committee of the Black Panther Party, *The Black Panther Black Community News Service* (Oakland: Black Panther Party, 1969), 7 June 1969, 23.

14. Carmichael and Hamilton, *Black Power*, 46–47.

Chapter 1

The epigraph to this chapter is from Elbert 'Big Man' Howard, "Remember Brother Malcolm," *Black Panther*, 19 May 1969, 4.

1. W. E. B. DuBois, The Souls of Black Folks (1903; reprint, New York: Bantam Books, 1989), 3–4. All page citations are to the reprint edition.

2. Malcolm X, *Ballots or Bullets*; Malcolm X, *Grass Roots Speech: Detroit, Michigan, November 10, 1963*, audio recording (New York: Paul Winley Records, 1963); Benjamin Karim, *The End of White World Supremacy: Four Speeches by Malcolm X* (New York: Arcade Publishing, 1971), 134–35. In these speeches Malcolm discusses how conventional politics had "betrayed" blacks and why they needed to identify as nationalists; "Remember the Words of Brother Malcolm," *Black Panther*, 18 May 1968, 6–7.

3. Malcolm X, *Ballots or Bullets*; Malcolm X, *Grass Roots Speech*; Karim, *End of White World Supremacy*, 134–35; American Communist William Patterson of the Civil Rights Congress also petitioned the UN in 1951 with his *We Charge Genocide* tract.

4. Landon Williams, interview on *Black Power, Black Panthers*, KQED, San Francisco, April 1990.

5. Timothy B. Tyson, *Radio Free Dixie: Robert F. Williams and the Roots of Black Power* (Chapel Hill: University of North Carolina Press, 1999), 79–89; Robert F. Williams, *Negroes with Guns* (Detroit: Wayne State University Press, 1998), 17–21.

6. Tyson, *Radio Free Dixie*, 149.

7. Ibid., 262–86.

8. Ibid.

9. "Remember the Words of Brother Malcolm," *Black Panther*, 20 July 1967, 8 ibid., 18 May 1968, 6–7; Earl Anthony, "Malcolm, Malcolm," *Black Panther*, 28 September 1968, 9; "Remember Brother Malcolm," 4–5; "Remember Malcolm," *Black Panther*, 15 May 1971, 16.

10. Anthony, "Malcolm, Malcolm," 9.

11. Kitamba Cah Chuma, "A Message to the Ghetto," *Black Panther*, 19 October 1968, 2; George Murray, "The Necessity of a Black Revolution," *Black Panther*, 16 November 1968, 13; Brother Dynamite, "Eldridge Cleaver: Takes Revolution Underground," *Black Panther* 7 December 1968, 2.

12. Seale, *Seize the Time*, 25, 26, 63.

13. Frantz Fanon, *The Wretched of the Earth* (New York: Grove Press, 1963), 35–106.

14. "White 'Mother Country' Radicals," *Black Panther*, 20 July 1967, 1.

15. Seale, *Seize the Time*, 64.

16. Earl Ofari, "The Last Thing We Need Is Rhetoric from K. Cleaver," *Los Angeles Free Press*, 30 October 1971, 27, in Huey P. Newton Foundation Collection, series 8, box 2, folder 22, Stanford University, Green Library, Department of Special Collections, M864.

17. Ibid. Ofari criticizes the BPP leadership for basing their organization on the underclass.

18. "Armed Black Brothers in the Black Community," *Black Panther*, 25 April 1967, 3; Huey Newton, "Fear and Doubt," *Black Panther*, 19 October 1968, 9; Cleaver, "On the Ideology of the Black Panther Party," 12–15.

19. Muhammad, *Message to the Blackman*, 161–64; Seale, *Seize the Time*, 66–69.

20. Mumia Abu Jamal, "A Life in the Party," in *Liberation, Imagination, and the Black Panther Party: A New Look at the Panthers and Their Legacy*, ed. Kathleen Cleaver and George Katsiaficas, 40–42 (New York: Routledge Press, 2001).

21. Huey Newton, "In Defense of Self-Defense: The Correct Handling of a Revolution, *Black Panther*, 20 July 1967, 3, 5.

22. David Hilliard and Lewis Cole, *This Side of Glory: The Autobiography of David Hilliard and the Story of the Black Panther Party* (Boston: Little, Brown and Co., 1993), 129.

23. "Panthers Ambushed—One Murdered," *Black Panther*, 4 May 1968, 4; Hilliard and Cole, *This Side of Glory*, 182–95.

24. Ofari, "Last Thing We Need."

25. Alex Haley, *The Autobiography of Malcolm X* (New York: Grove Press, 1965), 343–381–84.

26. "In Defense of Self-Defense: An Exclusive Interview with Minister of Defense, Huey P. Newton," *Black Panther*, 16 March 1968, 4, 16–18; "To Black Politicians: Political Consequences and Black Politicians," *Black Panther*, 16 March 1968, 2; Kathleen Cleaver, " sition of the Black Panther Party on the Seventh Congressional District Election in Alameda County and the Candidacy of John George in the Democratic Party," *Black Panther* March 1968, 2, 22; Eldridge Cleaver, "Black Paper by the Minister of Information," *Black Panther*, 4 May 1968, 12.

27. "Eldridge Cleaver for President, Kathleen Cleaver for Assemblywoman, Huey Newton for Congress, and Bobby Seale for Assemblyman," *Black Panther*, 18 May 1968, 17–

28. Louis Heath, ed., "Relations with Domestic Organizations," *Black Panthers Speak:*

Huey P. Newton, Bobby Seale, Eldridge and Company Speak Out through the Black Panther Party's Official Newspaper (Metuchen, N.J.: Scarecrow Press, 1976), 91–93, courtesy of the Bancroft Library, University of California-Berkeley.

29. "Young Patriots at UFAF Conference," *Black Panther*, 26 July 1969, 8; "Young Lords Organization," *Black Panther*, 18 October 1969, 3.

30. Huey P. Newton, "The Black Panthers," *Ebony*, August 1969, 106–13.

31. Malcolm X, *Ballots or Bullets*; Malcolm X, *Grass Roots Speech*.

32. Huey P. Newton, "In Defense of Self-Defense, II: July 3, 1967," in Hilliard and Weise, *Huey P. Newton Reader*, 138–41; Kathleen Cleaver, "Black Lawyers Are Jiving," *Black Panther*, 18 May 1968, 6.

33. Huey P. Newton, "Black Capitalism Re-Analyzed, I: June 5, 1971," Hilliard and Weise, *Huey P. Newton Reader*, 227–31.

34. Ibid.

35. Year 1973 review quiz no. 2 (quiz on the history of the black church, the development of black businesses and black capitalism reanalyzed, and the history of the Black Panther Party), Huey Newton Foundation Collection, series 2, subseries 2, box 4, folder 3, central committee information; "White 'Mother Country' Radicals," *Black Panther*, 20 July 1967, 1.

36. Linda Harrison, "On Cultural Nationalism," *Black Panther*, 2 February 1969, 2; Huey P. Newton, "To the Black Movement, May 15, 1968" in *To Die for the People*, 92–95; David Hilliard and Cole, *This Side of Glory*, 163, 170.

37. African Patriotic Armed Struggle Grows in Strength," *Black Panther*, 17 February 1969, 14; "The True Culture of Africa and Africans," *Black Panther*, 17 February 1969, 18.

38. Hilliard and Cole, *This Side of Glory*, 163, 170.

39. Ibid., 171–75; Chris Booker, "Lumpenization: A Critical Error of the Black Panther Party," in *Black Panther Party Reconsidered*, 351; Stokely Carmichael and Michael Thelwell, *Ready for Revolution: The Life and Struggles of Stokely Carmichael (Kwame Ture)* (New York: Scribner, 2003), 660–71.

40. Seale, *Seize the Time*, 29–34.

41. "Black Curriculum," *Black Panther*, 20 July 1967, 24; "Black Students Union Statewide High School Convention, October 26, 1968," *Black Panther*, 19 October 1968, 12; "10 Point Program and Platform of the Black Student Unions," *Black Panther*, 19 October 1968, 7.

42. Iris Wyse, "Black Curriculum," *Black Panther*, 12 October 1968, 17; "Black Liberation Publishers," *Black Panther*, 16 November 1968, 21; Sidney F. Walton, Jr., *The Black Curriculum: Developing a Program in Afro-American Studies* (East Palo Alto, Calif.: Black Liberation Publishers, 1969), 127–38.

43. "Black Student Revolutionary Conference, New Haven, Conn., May 16–May 19, 1970," *Black Panther*, 9 May 1970, 23.

44. Paul Fleming, "Merritt College Students Fail to Participate in the Breakfast Program," *Black Panther*, 25 May 1969, 5.

45. Earl Caldwell, "Panthers' Meeting Shifts Aims from Racial Confrontation to Class Struggle," *New York Times*, 22 July 1969, 21.

46. "Black Paper by the Minister of Information," *Black Panther*, 4 May 1968, 12. This

paper was presented to the founding convention of the Peace and Freedom Party. Cleaver call for an RPCC can be dated from at least this time. Cleaver discusses the BPP's reasons for making interracial coalitions. He also calls for revolution in the black community and the larger white society.

47. Black Panther Party, "Message to America: Delivered On the 107th Anniversary of the Emancipation Proclamation at Washington DC Capital of Babylon, World Racism, and Imperialism, June 19, 1970, by the Black Panther Party," *Black Panther,* 20 June 1970, centerfold. This manifesto served as the formal call for an RPCC and traces the evolution of BPP ideology from Black Nationalism to revolutionary nationalism.

48. Hilliard and Cole, *This Side of Glory,* 308.

49. Ibid.

50. Newton, "In Defense of Self-Defense," 3, 5.

51. Robert Terry and Charles Gilbert, "14 Panthers Seized in Raid Are Held on $100,000 Bail," *Philadelphia Inquirer,* 1 September 1970, 1; Denise Kirkland and James Lintz, "Panthers Reopen Offices, Vow to Hold Convention; 14 Suspects Lose Appeals," *Philadelphia Inquirer,* 2 September 1970, 1.

52. Dennis Kirkland and Hoag Levins, "Spirit of Peace Flows Freely at Panthers' Parley, *Philadelphia Inquirer,* 7 September 1970, 1; George Katsiaficas, "Organization and Movement: The Case of the Black Panther Party and the Revolutionary People's Constitutional Convention in 1970," in Cleaver and Katsiaficas, *Liberation, Imagination,* 141–55.

53. U.S. House of Representatives, *Gun-Barrel Politics,* 124–26.

54. Ibid, 126.

55. Hilliard and Cole, *This Side of Glory,* 319.

56. "Panthers Move Internationally: Free Huey at the UN," *Black Panther,* 14 September 1968, 3.

Chapter 2

The epigraph to this chapter is from "To Feed Our Children," *Black Panther,* 27 April 1969, 3.

1. Gwen V. Hodges, "Survival Pending Revolution," *Black Panther,* 9 January 1971, 3.

2. Newton, "On the Defection of Eldridge Cleaver."

3. Ibid.

4. Holder, "History of the Black Panther Party," 76–77; "Richmond Breakfast for Schoolchildren," *Black Panther Black Community News Service,* 31 March 1969, 9; "Harlem Free Breakfast Program," *Black Panther,* 7 June 1969, 20; "To Feed Our Children," *Black Panther,* 27 April 1969, 3.

5. Newton, "Black Panthers," 106.

6. Doug Miranda, interview with author, 8 October 2000; Landon Williams, interview with author, 9 October 2000.

7. "Warning to So-Called Paper Panthers," *Black Panther,* 14 September 1968, 10.

8. Landon Williams, interview; "Breakfast for School Children," *Black Panther,* 21 December 1968, 15.

9. Hilliard and Cole, *This Side of Glory,* 157, "Central Committee BPP Press Conference," *Black Panther,* 4 January 1969, 6; "Beware Of…," *Black Panther,* 9 March 1969, 7.

10. "Chairman Bobby Seale," *The Movement*, March 1969, reprinted in *Black Panther*, 3 March 1969, 11.

11. Ibid.

12. "Ten Years of Struggle, Ten Years of Service to the People," *Black Panther*, 19 October 1976, suppl., I; "Volunteers Needed," *Black Panther*, 19 October 1968, 2; ibid., 2 November 1968, 7; "Breakfast for School Children," 15.

13. "Vallejo Chapter Starts Breakfast for Children," *Black Panther*, 31 March 1969, 17; "Vallejo Chapter Expels Reactionaries," *Black Panther*, 31 March 1969, 17.

14. "Breakfast for Schoolchildren Programs," *Black Panther*, 1 November 1969, 20. Some scholars have cited earlier versions of the breakfast program during 1967 and 1968 in Seattle and the Bay Area. On page 17 of the November 15, 1969, issue of the BPP newspaper, however, the Seattle branch marked that month as the official opening of its breakfast program.

15. U.S. Senate, Committee to Study Government Operations, *Book 3: Final Report of the Select Committee to Study Government Operations with Respect to Intelligence Operations*, 94th Cong., 2nd sess. (Washington, D.C.: Government Printing Office, 1976), 210–11.

16. Ibid., 212.

17. "Des Moines Breakfast for Children Rally Attacked by Pigs," *Black Panther*, 27 April 1969, 4; "Fascist Pigs Ruined $300 Worth of Free Breakfast Food," *Black Panther*, 7 June 1969, 20; "Breakfast Sabotage," *Black Panther*, 15 November 1969, 17.

18. Abron, "Serving the People," 185.

19. Ibid.; "San Francisco Starts Liberation School," *Black Panther*, 2 August 1969, 14; "The Liberation School," *Black Panther*, 2 August 1969, 14.

20. "Staten Island Liberation School," *Black Panther*, 30 August 1969, 21.

21. Abron, "Serving the People," 186; 1977 brochure from the Oakland Community School; letter titled "About the Oakland Community School," Huey P. Newton Foundation Collection, series 2, subseries 3, box 16, folder 2; "Black Panther on Board," *Oakland Tribune*, 14 May 1976, 3; Huey P. Newton Foundation Collection, series 2, subseries 3, box 16, folder 1; undated brochure from the Community Learning Center and 23 August 1971 Intercommunal Youth Institute Planning Paper "Toward A True Education" from Hudson Papers, box 1, BPP Archives, Howard University, Moorland-Spingarn Research Center.

22. "Rules of the Black Panther Party," *Black Panther*, 7 June 1969, 23. Rule 24 prohibits chapters from accepting grants or any other money without first contacting national headquarters.

23. Oakland Community School, 1977 brochure; letter titled "About the Oakland Community School," Huey Newton Foundation Collection, series 2, subseries 3, box 16, folder 2; undated brochure from the Community Learning Center, Hudson Papers, box 1.

24. Abron, "Serving the People," 186.

25. Dr. Tolbert Small, memorandum to author, November 1990. Dr. Small was the national chairman of the BPP's Sickle Cell Anemia Project and also worked at the Bobby Seale People's Free Health Clinic in Berkeley.

26. "Bobby Hutton Free Health Clinic," *Black Panther*, 25 October 1969, 4; "Serving the People Medical Clinic," *Black Panther*, 30 August 1969, 16; Abron, "Serving the People," 184; Dr. Small, memorandum.

27. "Serving the People Medical Clinic," 16.

28. Assata Shakur, *Assata: An Autobiography* (Westport, Conn.: Lawrence Hill and Co., 1987), 217.

29. Holder, "History of the Black Panther Party," 113.

30. Ibid., 111–16.

31. Dr. Small, memorandum.

32. "Serving the People Medical Clinic," 16.

33. Ibid.; "Illinois Chapter Free Medical Clinic," *Black Panther*, 18 October 1969, 3.

34. Michael "Cetawayo" Tabor, *Capitalism Plus Dope Equals Genocide* (New York: Black Panther Party, 1970).

35. Dr. Small, memorandum.

36. "What Does the Decentralization of Police Mean?" *Black Panther*, 30 August 1969, 15.

37. "Black Panther Book List," *Black Panther*, 16 November 1968, 21.

38. Billy X, "When I Joined the Party—Panther in Training," *It's About Time*, Fall 2002, 11, http://www.itsabouttimebpp.com.

39. Frank Jones, "Tightening Up," *Black Panther*, 25 January 1969, 17; "Chairman Bobby Seale," 10.

40. Shakur, *Assata*, 221–22.

41. Ibid., 222.

42. Ibid., 221–23.

43. Bobby Seale, Ericka Huggins, and Michael Cross, "Political Education and the Renewal of the Ideological Institute" memo to the central body, 28 August 1973, Huey Newton Foundation Collection, series 2, subseries 2, box 4, folder 3.

44. "The Roots of the Party," *Black Panther*, 25 May 1969, 4.

45. Orientation lectures, Ideological Institute of the Black Panther Party, 12 and 19 December 1970, Huey P. Newton Foundation Collection, series 2, subseries 3, box 18, folder 11.

46. Kathleen Cleaver, "Back to Africa: The Evolution of the International Section of the Black Panther Party, 1969–1972," in Jones, *Black Panther Party Reconsidered*, 225.

47. "Breakfast for Schoolchildren Programs," 20; Abron, "Serving the People," 184–

48. "Hanrahan Seeks to Smash Black Youth," *Black Panther*, 28 March 1970, 8.

49. "Socialism: Serving the People," *Black Panther*, 1 November 1969, 19.

50. Cheryl Simmons, interview on *Black Power, Black Panthers*, KQED, San Francisco, 1990.

51. "Chairman Bobby Seale," 11.

52. Jimmy Slater, "Talking the Talk and Walkin' the Walk," interview, in *Black Panther Party Reconsidered*, 152.

53. Black Panther Party, *Fallen Comrades of the Black Panther Party* (Oakland, Calif.: Black Panther Party, 1973).

Chapter 3

The epigraph to this chapter is from "Freedom Fighters," editorial, *Black Panther*, 14 September 1968, 5.

1. U.S. House of Representatives, *Gun-Barrel Politics*, 69–80. There are no completely accurate figures for chapters or members. BPP membership was always in flux because chap-

ters were constantly opening and closing for a variety of reasons. Committee investigators claimed there were twenty-five chapters in 1968. They also said that by 1971 the BPP had operated at one time or another in sixty-one cities and twenty-six states. A chapter technically embraced an entire state, and a branch was a city within the state. Ollie Johnson states in *Black Panther Party Reconsidered* (p. 391) that there were BPP offices in forty cities by 1969. Personnel fluctuated due to purges, the 1971 schism, and the stresses of party life. There may have been five thousand members in 1968. J. Edgar Hoover testified in 1971 that there were forty-eight affiliates and that most were NCCFs. See Holder, "History of the Black Panther Party," 237.

2. Hilliard and Cole, *This Side of Glory*, 159.

3. U.S. House of Representatives, *Gun-Barrel Politics*, 71–72, 76–78; "Rules of the Black Panther Party," rules 20, 22, and 26.

4. U.S. House of Representatives, *Gun-Barrel Politics*, 72.

5. Ibid., 69–70.

6. Ibid., 69–80, 88–89; Holder, "History of the Black Panther Party," 236.

7. U.S. House of Representatives, *Gun-Barrel Politics*, 72.

8. Ibid., 77.

9. Ibid., 76–78; "Pigs Bomb Des Moines Panther Headquarters," *Black Panther*, 11 May 1969, 2; "Des Moines Panther Bombing," *Black Panther*, 19 May 1969, 15; "Omaha Purge" *Black Panther*, 21 June 1969, 11.

10. U.S. House of Representatives, *Gun-Barrel Politics*, 83–87.

11. U.S. Senate, *Book 3: Final Report*, 214; Karen Williams, memo to "Servant," i.e., Huey Newton, regarding distribution weekly report, 2 July 1972. Williams reports that fifty-two thousand papers have been ordered. The largest amount was 14,403 in Oakland, and the smallest amount was 867 for New Haven. Chicago sold 8,198 papers, and New York ordered 3,600, but there was no indication of how many were actually sold. The memo is also valuable for listing the functioning branches in 1972; see Huey Newton Foundation Collection, series 2, subseries 2, box 13, folder 10. In the 4 August 1978 editing cadre report, JoNina Abron states that fifty-five hundred papers cost $402.80 to print and that because of financial struggles the paper was often late. According to a 9 January 1979 memo from Abron to Newton regarding funding the paper, Los Angeles, Chicago, Detroit, and Milwaukee were the only cities still selling the paper; see Huey Newton Foundation Collection, series 2, subseries 2, box 13, folder 4.

12. U.S. House of Representatives, *Gun-Barrel Politics*, 83–87.

13. Tom Wolfe, *Radical Chic and Mau-Mauing the Flak Catchers* (New York: Farrar, Straus, and Giroux, 1970), 56–87; U.S. House of Representatives, *Gun-Barrel Politics*, 83–87. Committee investigators determined that Paul Moore III anonymously contributed $20,000 to the breakfast program but that the funds were used for Newton's bail (85).

14. U.S. House of Representatives, *Gun-Barrel Politics*, 83–87.

15. Eugene Williams, interview with author, Orinda, Calif., 1 March 2002; U.S. House of Representatives, *Gun-Barrel Politics*, 86–87; in 8 July 1972 memo from "The Servant," i.e., Newton, regarding "The Sale of Our Paper," Newton directs that members will receive ten cents for every paper they sell. See Huey Newton Foundation Collection, series 2, subseries 2, box 4, folder 14.

16. Lance Williams and Pearl Stewart, "Panthers' School Chief Sued," *Oakland Tribune* 10 November 1977, 1; Pearl Stewart, "Two Suspects in Panther Shooting Get City Pay, *Oakland Tribune*, 3 November 1977, 1; Abron Papers, BPP Archives; in 4 September 1977 memo from Darron Perkins (leader of the Chicago branch) to Newton, Perkins reports that the chapter had dwindled to seven members and that finances were based on college grants, scholarships, veterans' job-training programs, and manual labor. Members were seeking work as cooks, plumbers, and steelworkers (see Huey Newton Foundation Collection, series 2, subseries 2, box 5, folder 8).

17. "Rules of the Black Panther Party," rule 24, *Black Panther*, 28 March 1970, 18.

18. Agenda notes from central body meeting relating to an internal audit, 15 September 1979, Huey Newton Foundation Collection, series 2, subseries 2, box 4, folder 6.

19. U.S. House of Representatives, *Gun-Barrel Politics*, 80; in Shakur, *Assata*, 216 Shakur describes how she walked into the office and began working on organizational fi the Revolutionary People's Constitutional Convention, and the community programs.

20. I met Carl Hampton in 1969 when he stopped me on the street and asked directions to BPP national headquarters in Berkeley. Hampton had played saxophone in a band but left because he wanted to be a Panther. Carl Hampton was an honest and brave young man who exemplified the Panther rank and file's sacrifice and devotion to duty.

21. "Black Amnesty among People's Party II Goals," *Houston Chronicle*, 27 July 1970, 2.

22. Thomas Wright, "Who Fingered Carl Hampton?" *Sepia*, November 1970, 8–13; " lice, Militants Blame Each Other," *Dallas Morning News*, 27 July 1970, 5A; "Black Leader Dies at Second Run-In," *Dallas Morning News*, 28 July 1970, 19A; George Rosenblatt and Steve Singer, "Police, Gunmen Exchange Fire; 52 Are Arrested, *Houston Chronicle*, 27 July 1970, 1; Jim Barlow, "Police Say Militants Began Houston Fight," *Dallas Morning News* July 1970, 1.

23. "Black Group Wants Ouster of Chief Short," *Houston Chronicle*, 28 July 1970, 1.

24. "BPP Trains Houstonians for Free Medical Testing Program," *Black Panther*, 22 June 1974, 5.

25. Bob Poole, "FBI Tied to Panther Smear Here," *Winston-Salem Journal*, 12 December 1975, 1; Jack Betts, "Files Point to Harassment of Winston Group," *Greensboro Daily News* n.d., A1; Huey Newton Foundation Collection, series 2, subseries, 8 box 49, folder 3; Bill Bancroft, "The Black Panthers Today," *Twin City Sentinel*, week of 12 May 1972, feature page; Huey Newton Foundation Collection, series 8, box 4, folder 5. These articles document the FBI's activity against the North Carolina Panthers; North Carolina newspaper ures differ from the BPP's because an internal party memo put paper sales at 1,000 sold out of 1,063 issues ordered. Karen Williams, memo to the "Servant," i.e., Newton, 2 July 1972, Huey Newton Foundation Collection, series 2, subseries 8, box 13, folder 10; "Winston-Salem Free Ambulance Service Opens," *Black Panther*, 16 February 1974, 3.

26. Poole, "FBI Tied to Panther Smear Here," 1; Betts, "Files Point to Harassment of Winston Group," A1; Huey Newton Foundation Collection, series 2, subseries 8, box 49, folder 3; Bancroft, "Black Panthers Today"; Huey Newton Foundation Collection, series 8, box 4, folder 5.

27. Betsy Halstead, "NCCF Moves Headquarters," *New Orleans Times-Picayune*, 25 October 1970, sec. 1, p. 20.

28. Don Hughes, "Two Badly Beaten Spies Recall Horrors of Panther Justice," *New Orleans Times-Picayune*, 19 September 1970, 1.

29. "Eleven Are Shot; Sixteen Arrested," *New Orleans Times-Picayune*, 16 September 1970, 1; James H. Gillis, "Rights Denied Violence Issue," *New Orleans Times-Picayune*, 17 September 1970, 1; "Police, Hold It Don't Do It, Said Warning to Victims," *New Orleans Times-Picayune*, 17 September 1970, 1; "Available Reports Are Being Studied," *New Orleans Times-Picayune*, 18 September 1970, 1.

30. "Desire Incident Probe Is Slated," *New Orleans Times-Picayune*, 15 October 1970, sec. 6, p. 5; Betsy Halstead, "No Fire Bomb Probers Told," *New Orleans Times-Picayune*, 17 October 1970, sec. 3, p. 3.

31. Halstead, "NCCF Moves Headquarters," 20; "Officials Study Action by NCCF," *New Orleans Times-Picayune*, 28 October 1970, 1; NCCF's Eviction Is Being Sought," *New Orleans Times-Picayune*, 30 October 1970, sec. 4, p. 23; in K. Williams, memo to Newton regarding distribution weekly report, 2 July 1972, New Orleans is not listed as a chapter selling any papers; see Huey Newton Foundation Collection, series 2, subseries 8, box 13, folder 10.

32. "Statement on Renegade Provocateur Agent Tommy Jones," *Black Panther*, 20 April 1969, 7; "Indiana Chapter Purges," *Black Panther*, 20 April 1969, 7.

33. Jeanne F. Theoharris and Komozi Woodard, *Freedom North: Black Freedom Struggles outside the South, 1940–1980* (New York: Palgrave: 2003), 50–51.

34. Holder, "History of the Black Panther Party," 230; Hilliard and Cole, *This Side of Glory*, 226–32; "Illinois Chapter Free Medical Clinic," *Black Panther*, 18 October 1969, 3.

35. Theoharris and Woodard, *Freedom North*, 58.

36. Heath, *Black Panther Leaders Speak*, 91–93, courtesy of Bancroft Library, University of California-Berkeley; Hilliard and Cole, *This Side of Glory*, 229–30.

37. "Young Lords Organization: Pigs Block 'Cha Cha' Jiminez," *Black Panther*, 18 October 1969, 3.

38. "SDS: A Need for Revolutionary Line," *Black Panther*, 18 October 1969, 3.

39. U.S. Senate, *Book 3: Final Report*, 195–99; Hilliard and Cole, *This Side of Glory*, 228–29.

40. "Hanrahan Seeks to Smash Black Youth," 8.

41. Louis Heath, ed., *Off the Pigs! The History and Literature of the Black Panther Party* (Metuchen, N.J.: Scarecrow Press, 1976), 178–80, courtesy of Bancroft Library, University of California-Berkeley.

42. Black Panther Party, Illinois Chapter, "Statement to the People on the Assassination of Fred Hampton and Mark Clark," *Ministry of Information Bulletin*, n.d., 1; Black Panther Party, Illinois Chapter, "When One of Us Falls, 1,000 Will Take His Place," *Rockford Branch Newsletter*, n.d., 1 (copies in possession of author).

43. Hilliard and Cole, *This Side of Glory*, 268–70, 277.

44. "Panther Spy Dies," *Washington Afro-American*, 27 January 1990, n.p., Hudson Papers, box 2; "FBI Role Exposed in Fred Hampton Murder," *Black Panther*, 8 June 1974, 3.

45. Hilliard and Cole, *This Side of Glory*, 371–72; Darron Perkins, memo to Newton, 4 September 1977. Perkins (leader of the Chicago office) reported on the membership and financial status of the chapter; see Huey Newton Foundation Collection, series 2, subseries 2, box 5, folder 8.

46. Holder, "History of the Black Panther Party," 231–32; U.S. House of Representatives, *Gun-Barrel Politics*, 60–63; "New Pig Patrol in Kansas City," *Black Panther*, 20 April 1969, 18.

47. "KC Press Release," "Ambush," and "Seat of Fascism," all from *Black Panther*, 25 October 1969, 4.

48. "People's Demonstration against Filth," *Black Panther*, 21 June 1969, 11; "Bobby Hutton Free Health Clinic," 4.

49. Charlotte Hill O'Neal, "The Blessings of Water," *It's About Time*, Fall 2002, 2, http://www.itsabouttimebpp.com.

50. Heath, *Off the Pigs*, 184; U.S. House of Representatives, *Gun-Barrel Politics*, 77, 121.

51. Billy Murray, Tom Nugent, and William Schmidt, "Policeman Slain Near Home Reported as Panther Office," *Detroit Free Press*, 25 October 1970, 1; "15 Accused in Police Killing: Surrender after Long Siege," *Detroit Free Press*, 26 October 1970, 2A; William Schmidt, "Dynamite Is Found in Panther House," *Detroit Free Press*, 27 October 1970, 1; Hugh Morgan, "Officer's Death Charged to 15," *New Orleans Times-Picayune*, 26 October 1970, 1.

52. U.S. House of Representatives, *Gun-Barrel Politics*, 81–82. Former Seattle Panthers testifying during House Internal Security Committee hearings alleged they were ordered to commit robberies to fund guerilla warfare efforts. There were also allegations that sniping at police officers was encouraged; Heath, *Off The Pigs*, 184; Robert Sweet, "Girl Panther Raps about Revolution," article from an unidentified Seattle newspaper describes how a panther joined the Seattle office and what her daily activities were; see Huey Newton Foundation Collection, series 8, box 4, folder 4.

53. U.S. House of Representatives, *Gun-Barrel Politics*, 82.

54. "Letter from Seattle Panthers," *Black Panther*, 16 November 1969, 16; "Seattle BPP Holds Thanksgiving Feast," *Black Panther*, 8 December 1973, 3.

55. Sweet, "Girl Panther Raps."

56. Hilliard and Cole, *This Side of Glory*, 164, 234; Akinyele Umoja, "Repression Breeds Resistance: The Black Liberation Army and the Radical Legacy of the Black Panther Party, in Cleaver and Katsiaficas, *Liberation, Imagination*; Cleaver and Katsiaficas, *Liberation, Imagination*, 6–7; Brown, *Taste of Power*, 141–46. Umoja and Brown state that Carter referred to his underground organization as the "wolves."

57. Claude Andrew Clegg III, *An Original Man: The Life and Times of Elijah Muhammad* (New York: St. Martin's Press, 1997), 88–97.

58. Ibid., 96.

59. George L. Jackson, *Blood in My Eye* (Baltimore: Black Classic Press, 1990), ix–xviii.

60. Ibid., xviii.

61. Ibid., ix–xiii, 74.

62. According to Robert Williams, "We have to wage a struggle inside the jails and prisons, simultaneous with the struggles in the streets"; see *Black Panther*, 26 December 1970, 8.

63. Al Armour, "Letters to the People from Prisoners of War, So. Calif. Chapter of the Black Panther Party," *Black Panther*, 26 December 1970, 8; "Let the Madmen Out," *Black*

Panther, 26 December 1970, 8; "We Will Free Ourselves," *Black Panther*, 26 December 1970, 8; "Free Ruchell Magee," *Black Panther*, 6 February 1971, 10–11.

64. Jackson, *Blood in My Eye*, xiv–xv.

65. Robert Popp, "Judge and Cons Slain—Photo Story of Battle," *San Francisco Chronicle*, 8 August 1970, 1.

66. "The San Quentin Branch of the Black Panther Party Opens," *Black Panther*, 27 February 1971, 10–11; Larry D. Hatfield, "3 Guards, 3 Cons Slain in Quentin Breakout Try," *San Francisco Chronicle*, 22 August 1971, 1; Ed Montgomery, "Toy Pistols Found on Kin in 'Dry Run,'" *San Francisco Examiner*, 23 August 1971, 1.

67. Ed Montgomery, "Black Militant Now Fed Up Tells Story," *San Francisco Sunday Examiner and Chronicle*, 26 March 1972, 6, sec. A.

68. U.S. House of Representatives, *Gun-Barrel Politics*, 88; Shakur, *Assata*, 181–82.

69. "New York Breakfast for Children," *Black Panther*, 7 June 1969, 20; "Serving the People Medical Clinic," *Black Panther*, 30 August 1969, 16; "Staten Island Liberation School," 21; "NY Free Clothes," *Black Panther*, 1 November 1969, 19; "Attention to the Black Community," *Black Panther*, 6 June 1970, 16; Holder, "History of the Black Panther Party," 271. Holder states that in a two-week period in 1969, the New York City chapter sold 35,000 of the national run of 108,000 papers.

70. Holder, "History of the Black Panther Party," 266.

71. Ibid., 260–61.

72. Ibid., 265–66.

73. Ibid., 272–73, 277; New York 21, "Open Letter to the Weather Underground," 3.

74. New York 21, *Look for Me in the Whirlwind: The Collective Autobiography of the New York 21* (New York: Vintage Books, 1971), 363–64. Fifteen Panthers were brought to trial. Three were never apprehended, two were severed from the case due to their youth, and one was severed because of illness; Joel Dreyfuss, "Defense Labels Panther Trial 'Most Controversial,'" *New Orleans Times-Picayune*, 19 October 1970, sec. 2, 12; Hilliard and Cole, *This Side of Glory*, 168. The cultural differences between New York and California are also discussed by Holder in his dissertation ("History of the Black Panther Party," 261); Edith Evans Asbury, "Agent Testifies of Panther's Escape," *New York Times*, 5 March 1971, 28; Donald Flynn, "Panther Jurors: Prosecution Did Not Prove It," *New York Daily News*, 15 May 1971, 7.

75. Shakur, *Assata*, 227.

76. "A 'Most Wanted' Is Slain," *San Francisco Chronicle*, 15 November 1973, 25; Cleaver and Katsiaficas, *Liberation, Imagination*, 13.

77. "Black Groups Operating in Phila.," *Philadelphia Inquirer*, 7 September 1970, 5; Leonard J. McAdams, "Black Panthers Few but Feared and the Phila. Chapter Is Growing," *Philadelphia Inquirer*, 1 September 1970, 13.

78. Terry and Gilbert, "14 Panthers Seized in Raid," 1; "Four Seized, 3 Sought in Police Killing," *Philadelphia Inquirer*, 1 September 1970, 4; Dennis Kirkland and James Lintz, "Panthers Reopen Offices, Vow to Hold Convention, 14 Suspects Lose Appeals," *Philadelphia Inquirer*, 2 September 1970, 1; Edward Shapiro, "Citizens Objecting to Raids by Police," *Philadelphia Inquirer*, 2 September 1970, 3; Anthony Lame, "Panther Denies Know-

ing 7 Suspects in Slaying," *Philadelphia Inquirer*, 3 September 1970, 1; "Report of Panther Weapons Led to Raids, Rizzo Says," *Philadelphia Inquirer*, 4 September 1970, 1.

79. Edward Eisen, "Court Puts Restraints on Police," *Philadelphia Inquirer*, 5 September 1970, 1; Dennis Kirkland and William Thompson, "Hundreds Gather in Phila. for Panthers Convention," *Philadelphia Inquirer*, 5 September 1970, 1; Thomas J. Madden, "Newton Hails 'New Day Dawning,'" *Philadelphia Inquirer*, 6 September 1970, 1; Dennis Kirkland, David Umansky, and Cliff Linedecker, "Words Hot, People Cool at Temple," *Philadelphia Inquirer*, 6 September 1970, 1; Dennis Kirkland and Hoag Levins, "Spirit of Peace Flows Freely at Panthers' Parley," *Philadelphia Inquirer*, 7 September 1970, 1; Acel Moore and John Clancy, "Revolutionaries Reassert Goals as Parley Ends," *Philadelphia Inquirer*, 8 September 1970, 1; Acel Moore, "Only a Start, Radicals Say of Work Here," *Philadelphia Inquirer* September 1970, 10; David Umansky, "Whites Constitute 40 Pct. Attendance at Black Convention," *Philadelphia Inquirer*, 6 September 1970, 9.

80. Charyn Sutton, "2000 Blacks Meet in Atlanta," *Philadelphia Inquirer*, 6 September 1970, 9.

81. Harold Cruse, *The Crisis of the Negro Intellectual* (New York: William Morrow and Co.: 1967), 181–89.

82. Karen Williams, memo to "Servant," i.e., Huey Newton, 2 July 1972. Williams states that Philadelphia had ordered 2,036 papers and sold 1,254; Huey Newton Foundation Collection, series 2, subseries 2, box 13, folder 10. "Projects Outline-Item," 9A, 24 August 1977, 3. Item states all offices will be closed in two months. Huey Newton Foundation Collection, series 2, subseries 2, box 4, folder 6.

83. Yohuru Williams, *Black Politics/White Power: Civil Rights, Black Power, and the Black Panthers in New Haven* (St. James, N.Y.: Brandywine Press, 2000), 128.

84. Ibid., 131–45.

85. Ibid., 141–43.

86. Ibid.

87. "Minister of Education Returns from Cuba," *Black Panther*, 14 September 1968, 5; U.S. House of Representatives, *Gun-Barrel Politics*, 36. The committee report claims that when Murray was in Cuba he told the journal *Granma* that black Americans were inspired by the guerilla leader Che Guevera.

88. Tyson, *Radio Free Dixie*, 287–95.

89. Georgie Anne Geyer and Keyes Beech, "Black Idealistic Dream Shattered," *New Orleans Times-Picayune*, 21 October 1970, 1 (reprint from the Chicago Daily News Service). This is a fine series of articles about relations between African Americans and the Cuban revolution. Robert Williams returned to the United States in September 1969. He later gave an interview with Geyer and provided some insight about the difficulties faced by the Cubans as they tried to uphold their revolutionary credentials and rebuild their society.

90. Georgie Anne Geyer and Keyes Beech, "Black Militants Irk Fidel Castro," *New Orleans Times-Picayune*, 22 October 1970, 1; "Army Spied on King Family and Others for 75 Years," *Oakland Tribune*, 21 March 1993, 1. These articles explored relations with the Cubans and discussed other topics such as domestic spying by the American government. The *Times-Picayune* article also corroborates assertions made in the *Oakland Tribune* about guerilla training camps in Cuba.

91. Eric Pace, "African Nations Open 12-Day Cultural Festival with Parade through Algiers," *New York Times*, 22 July 1969, 9; Cleaver, "Back to Africa," 212, 217.

92. Cleaver, "Back to Africa," 213–30.

93. U.S. House of Representatives, *Gun-Barrel Politics*, 103; Cleaver, "Back to Africa," 230–34; "Cleaver and Black Panther Group Attend Hanoi Observance," *New York Times*, 19 August 1970, 13; Sanche de Gramont, "Our Other Man in Algiers," *New York Times Magazine*, 1 November 1970, 30, 112–27.

94. Cleaver, "Back to Africa," 235.

95. Ibid., 236–39; Hilliard and Cole, *This Side of Glory*, 268.

96. Cleaver, "Back to Africa," 245–49.

97. Ibid., 245–49; "Panther Villa Raid," *Los Angeles Herald Examiner*, 11 August 1972, 1; "Algeria: Panthers on Ice," *Time*, 4 September 1972, 32; "The Black Panthers Have Vanished from Algeria," *San Francisco Chronicle*, 29 March 1973, 19; Neal Ascherson, "Cleaver May Ask Asylum in France," *New York Post*, 2 April 1973, n.p., Huey Newton Foundation Collection, series 8, box 2, folder 22.

98. "Panther's Booklet Tells of SF Police Killing," *San Francisco Chronicle*, undated article but probably from 1971 or 1972. It discusses Cox's fifty-one-page booklet titled *On Organizing Urban Guerilla Units*. The booklet was allegedly written in Algiers in the fall of 1970, and it describes how Cox and five others ambushed housing authority policemen in 1967. San Francisco police say the case is still open. Huey Newton Foundation Collection, series 8, box 3, folder 18; Hilliard and Cole, *This Side of Glory*, 129. Hilliard and Cole make the same claim regarding Cox.

99. Hilliard and Cole, *This Side of Glory*, 307–8. All party finances were consolidated into Stronghold Productions. Huey Newton Foundation Collection, series 2, subseries 7, box 45, folders 1 and 6, contain a variety of legal instruments documenting the financial arrangements between the BPP and George Jackson and later his family concerning the rights to his writings.

100. "Projects Outline" agenda item 9A, 24 August 1977, 3, states that Newton will order all remaining offices closed by October 1977. Huey Newton Foundation Collection, series 2, subseries 2, box 4, folder 6.

101. Johnson, "Explaining the Demise," 404. Johnson describes how Seale and regional leaders unsuccessfully remonstrated with Newton in 1973 about the strategic error of closing local offices with thriving programs.

Chapter 4

The epigraph to this chapter is from New York 21, "An Open Letter to the People from 'Bobby Hutton,'" *Right On!*, 3 April 1971, 8, Wisconsin State Historical Society.

1. "A Call to Dissolve the Central Committee" and "Editorial," *Right On! Black Community News Service*, 3 April 1971, 2, Wisconsin State Historical Society.

2. Richard "Dharuba" Moore, "A Black Panther Speaks," *New York Times*, 12 May 1971, 43C.

3. Hodges, "Survival Pending Revolution," 3.

4. "Guerilla Acts of Sabotage and Terrorism in the United States, 1965–1970," reprinted from Scanlon's in *Black Panther*, 9 January 1971, 15.

5. "On the Purge of Geronimo Pratt from the Black Panther Party," *Black Panther* January 1971, 7; Umoja, "Repression Breeds Resistance," 8–15.

6. Jack Olson, *Last Man Standing: The Tragedy and Triumph of Geronimo Pratt* (New York: Doubleday Press, 2000), 69–99.

7. Roy Haynes, "Panther Slaying May Be Start of Cleaver-Newton Showdown," *Angeles Times*, November 1971; "Panther Factions Fight in Court," *San Francisco Examiner* 16 November 1971, 2; "2 Panther Factions in Court Brawl," *San Francisco Chronicle*, 16 November 1971, 3; Huey P. Newton Foundation Collection, series 8, box 2, folder 22.

8. Huey P. Newton, *Revolutionary Suicide* (New York: Harcourt Brace Jovanovich, 1973), 301–3; "Open Letter to the Weather Underground," 3; Umoja, "Repression Breeds Resistance," 8–15.

9. Cleaver, "On the Ideology of the Black Panther Party," 12–15.

10. George Rhodes, "Cleaver, Newton Split over Panther Purges," *San Francisco Examiner*, 26 February 1971, 1; "Newton Expels 14 Black Panthers," *San Francisco Examiner* 11 February 1971, 1.

11. "Enemies of the People," *Black Panther*, 13 February 1971, 12.

12. Earl Caldwell, "Internal Dispute Rends Panthers," *New York Times*, 7 March 1971, 26; "Free Kathleen Cleaver," *Black Panther Intercommunal News Service*, 6 March 1971, suppl., B–C; "Panthers Accuse Cleaver of Holding Wife in Algeria," *New York Times*, 5 March 1971, 28.

13. Newton, "On the Defection of Eldridge Cleaver," C–F.

14. Ibid.

15. "To Eldridge Cleaver and Conspirators from the San Quentin Branch of the Black Panther Party," *Black Panther*, 20 March 1971, 10–11.

16. "Rules of the Black Panther Party," number 6, *Black Panther*, 7 June 1969, 23.

17. Umoja, "Repression Breeds Resistance," 3–15.

18. "Last Warning: Attention, Pimps-Ho's-Dope Pushers," undated 1971 San Francisco flyer, Huey P. Newton Foundation Collection, series 2, subseries 2, box 11, folder 11.

19. Shakur, *Assata*, 231–36.

20. Ibid., 237–43.

21. Umoja, "Repression Breeds Resistance," 13–15.

22. "Brink's Case Shootout—Gunman Slain," *San Francisco Chronicle*, 24 October 1981, 1; "Bay Area Link to the Brink's Murder Case," *San Francisco Chronicle*, 24 October 1981, 2; "A 'Most Wanted' Is Slain," *San Francisco Chronicle*, 15 November 1973, 25.

23. "Statement by the Young Lords Party on the Split within the Black Panther Party," undated spring 1971 YLP leaflet, Huey Newton Foundation Collection, series 2, subseries 2, box 11, folder 10.

24. Ibid.

25. Ibid.

26. Robert C. Evans, letter to Newton, 15 April 1971, Huey Newton Foundation Collection, series 2, subseries 2, box 6, folder 5.

27. "Military Spy Network Dates Back to 1917," *Oakland Tribune*, 22 March 1993, A8,

reprinted from *Memphis Commercial-Appeal*, 6 August 1919; Walter Loving, "Final Report on Negro Subversion," 15 August 1919; and J. E. Cutler, "Memorandum for the Director of Military Intelligence," all in Walter H. Loving Papers, Moorland-Spingarn Research Center, Howard University, Washington, D.C.; David Levering Lewis, *W. E. B. DuBois: Biography of a Race, 1868–1919* (New York: Henry Holt and Co., 1993), 552–60.

28. Memo, FBI director to all offices, on Counter-Intelligence Program, Black Nationalist Hate Groups, Internal Security, 25 August 1967; FBI memo, G. C. Moore to W. C. Sullivan, on Counter-Intelligence Program, Black Nationalist Hate Groups, Racial Intelligence, 14 May 1970, *Counter-Intelligence Program of the FBI*.

29. U.S. Senate, *Book 3: Final Report*, 188–94; "FBI Plotting Led to Black Bloodletting," *San Francisco Examiner*, 26 May 1976, 1.

30. U.S. Senate, *Book 3: Final Report*, 188–94.

31. Ibid.

32. Brown, *Taste of Power*, 142–44, 164–70, 176–78.

33. U.S. Senate, *Book 3: Final Report*, 192–93; Ronald J. Ostrow and Narda Zacchino, "FBI Claimed Credit in 1969 for San Diego Ghetto War," *Los Angeles Times*, 4 January 1976, 8; Huey Newton Foundation Collection, series 2, subseries 8, box 49, folder 3; "San Diego Panther Murdered by Pork Chop Pigs," *Black Panther*, 31 May 1969, 18.

34. U.S. Senate, *Book 3: Final Report*, 200–207; C. Gerald Fraser, "FBI Files Reveal Moves against Black Panthers," *New York Times,* 19 October 1980, 1.

35. U.S. Senate, *Book 3: Final Report*, 199–200.

36. Ibid., 195–98.

37. Ibid., 209.

38. Ibid., 213, 218–20.

39. Seymour Hersh, "CIA Reportedly Recruited Blacks for Surveillance of Panther Party," *New York Times*, 17 March 1971, 1.

40. Ibid.; U.S. Senate, *Book 3: Final Report*, 252–54.

41. Huey P. Newton, "Executive Mandate No. 3," *Black Panther*, 16 March 1968, 1; Newton, "Black Panthers," 107–12.

42. U.S. Senate, *Book 3: Final Report*, 214.

43. "Radicals: Destroying the Panther Myth," *Time*, 22 March 1971, 20; Huey P. Newton Foundation Collection, series 8, box 2, folder 22.

44. "Remember Brother Malcolm," 4–5; "Roots of the Party," 4; Landon Williams, interview, Cheryl Simmons, interview, and JoNina Abron, interview, all from *Black Power, Black Panthers*, KQED, April 1990.

45. Fred Bennett, "As Black Panther Members," *Black Panther*, 21 December 1968, 15; "Breakfast for Schoolchildren Programs," 20; Black Panther Party, "What We Want," 21.

46. Eugene Williams, interview.

47. Ibid.

48. Ibid.

49. Ibid.; "A Strike for Self-Determination," *Black Panther*, 6 February 1971, 4; "Merritt College Strikes," *Black Panther*, 3 March 1971, 3.

50. Ed Montgomery, "$650 a Month, 25th Floor Digs," *San Francisco Examiner*, 12 February 1971, 1.

51. Eugene Williams, interview; U.S. Senate, *Book 3: Final Report*, 219.

52. "Pigs Threaten Well Being of the Supreme Servant of the People," *Black Panther* February 1971, 2.

53. Gayle and Andrew Glace, letter to Newton, 13 March 1971, and Kathryn A. Read, letter to Newton, 20 February 1971, Huey P. Newton Foundation Collection, series 1, sub-series 2, box 6, folder 5; "Huey Newton's Plush Pad a Gross Distortion," *San Francisco Sun Reporter*, 2 February 1971, reprinted in *Black Panther*, 27 February 1971, 5.

54. Eugene Williams, interview.

55. Ibid.

56. Ibid.

57. The statement, signed by Emory Douglas, Masai Hewitt, Big Man, Bob Rush, and Doug Miranda, stated, "We stand rock firm behind the BPP, our beloved and courageous central committee and our leader, Minister of Defense and Supreme Servant of the People, Huey P. Newton." See *Black Panther*, 20 March 1971, 12.

58. "Probation for a Former Radical," *San Francisco Chronicle*, 29 January 1972, 3; Huey Newton Foundation Collection, series 8, box 2, folder 1.

59. "Probation for a Former Radical," 3.

60. Joe Robertson, interview with author, 12 March 2002, Berkeley, Calif.

61. Ibid.

62. Hilliard and Cole, *This Side of Glory*, 129, 299–300, 310–12, 318; Central Committee of the Black Panther Party (Field Marshals Underground), *Black Panther*, 7 June 1969, 23.

63. Carlos Marighela, *Minimanual of the Urban Guerrilla* (Havana: Tricontinental Press, 1969), 6–7, 37–38.

64. Newton, "In Defense of Self-Defense," 3.

65. Newton, "Executive Mandate No. 3," 1; "Organizing Self-Defense Groups, Part 3, *Black Panther*, 30 January 1971, 7.

66. Umoja, "Repression Breeds Resistance," 8–9.

67. Eugene Williams, interview.

68. Robertson, interview.

69. "A Call to Dissolve the Central Committee," 2; "On the Assassination of Deputy Field Marshall Robert Webb," 3; "An Open Letter to the People from 'Bobby Hutton, and Michael "Cetewayo" Tabor, "On the Contradictions within the Black Panther Party, all in *Right On! Black Community News Service*, 3 April 1971, Wisconsin State Historical Society.

70. "Call to Dissolve the Central Committee," 2; Tabor, "On the Contradictions," 3.

71. "Radicals: "Destroying the Panther Myth," Huey P. Newton Foundation Collection, series 8, box 2, folder 22; "Circulate to Educate" and "For Sam," *Black Panther*, 8 May 1971, 8; "Death Here Tied to Panther Feud," *New York Times*, 10 March 1971, 29.

72. Robertson, interview; Eugene Williams, interview.

73. Robertson, interview; Eugene Williams, interview.

74. Carol Rucker, interview with author, 28 October 1990; Paul Alkebulan, "Power to the People: The Black Panther Party, 1966 to 1971" (master's project, California State University-Hayward, 1991).

75. Rucker, interview.

76. Black Panther Party, *Fallen Comrades.*

77. Edward Jay Epstein, "A Reporter at Large, The Panthers and the Police: A Pattern of Genocide?" *New Yorker*, 13 February 1971, 45–78.

78. "Updated List of Distress Signals," undated, Huey P. Newton Foundation Collection, series 2, subseries 2, box 4, folder 4.

79. Brown, *Taste Of Power*, 275, 350–52; Hilliard and Cole, *This Side of Glory*, 234–35.

80. Eugene Williams, interview.

Chapter 5

The epigraph to this chapter is from "The Black Liberation Struggle and Black Women," *Right On!* 19–31 December 1971, 11, in the Bloom Alternative Press Collection, box R4, Amherst College Archives and Special Collections, Amherst, Massachusetts.

1. "Skills Surveys," internal documents, central committee, Huey Newton Foundation Collection, series 2, subseries 2, box 4, folder 4. The dates on the 119 surveys are either January or February 1973. The majority were completed in 1973. Ericka Huggins, memo to June Hilliard, 1 November 1972, Huey Newton Foundation Collection, series 2, subseries 2, box 4, folder 4. This document verifies that another survey was done in November 1972 but does not say how many people were polled. The information in the memo summarized the raw data.

2. Muhammad, *Message to the Blackman*, 58–60; C. Eric Lincoln, *The Black Muslims in America* (Boston: Beacon Press, 1961), 31, 32, 83.

3. Brown, *Taste of Power*, 108–10.

4. Newton "Fear and Doubt," 9; "Armed Black Brothers in Richmond Community," *Black Panther*, 25 April 1967, 3.

5. Brown, *Taste of Power*, 326. Brown reveals that she helped Newton "painstakingly" write his book dedications in Ottawa.

6. Eldridge Cleaver, *Soul On Ice* (New York: Delta, 1968), 176–90.

7. Judy Hart, "Black Womanhood No. 1," *Black Panther*, 20 July 1967, 11.

8. "Black Woman," *Black Panther*, 14 September 1968, 6.

9. Linda Greene, "The Black Revolutionary Woman," *Black Panther*, 28 September 1968, 11; Gloria Bartholomew, "A Black Woman's Thoughts," *Black Panther*, 28 September 1968, 11.

10. Bruce Perry, ed., *Malcolm X: The Last Speeches* (New York: Pathfinder Press, 1989), 96, 98–99.

11. Martin Smith, "Capital Gun-Toters Draw Solons' Fury," *Sacramento Bee*, 3 May 1967, 1; "Police Arrest 24 Capital Invaders, Get 11 Weapons," *Sacramento Bee*, 3 May 1967, A4; Seale, *Seize the Time*, 153.

12. Tarika Lewis, interview with author, 13 October 1990, Oakland, Calif.; "The Black Panthers: The Historical Legacy" was sponsored by the Graduate Assembly of the University of California, 25–26 October 1990. The conference videotape, *The Black Panthers: Voices of Panther Women* (Berkeley, Calif.: Media Resources Center), features a panel discussion by six female party members; Carlos Hoffman, "Women Recount Role in Panther Party," *Daily Californian*, 29 October 1990, 7.

13. "Editorial Staff of the Black Panther, Ass't Revolutionary Artist: Matilaba, Editorial Ass't: Linda Boston," *Black Panther*, 19 October 1968, 7, 13; "Panther Sisters on Women's Liberation" (leaflet, 1969; repr., Heath, *Off the Pigs*, 339–41), courtesy of the Bancroft Library, University of California-Berkeley; Brown, *Taste of Power*, 189–92. According to Brown, she became part of a Los Angeles group known as the "clique," who were opposed to an inferior role for women in the BPP.

14. Eldridge Cleaver, "Message to Sister Ericka Huggins of the Black Panther Party, *Black Panther*, 5 July 1969, 16.

15. New York 21, *Look For Me in the Whirlwind*, 287–95, 303–9, 317–26; Seale, *Seize the Time*, 398; "Female Panther Tortured," *Black Panther*, 2 February 1969, 7; "Student Nurse Tortured," *Black Panther*, 17 February 1969, 9.

16. Imani Henry, "Black Liberation Army Soldier Speaks," *Worker's World News Service* 1 September 2002, pt. 2, 2.

17. Ibid.

18. Ibid., 3–10; Assata Shakur, "Message of Condolences on the Transition of Our Revolutionary Sista, Comrade, and Friend Safiya Bukhari," Havana, Cuba, August 29, 2003, *It's About Time*, 9 April 2005, http://www.itsabouttimebpp.com; Henry, "Black Liberation Army, passim.

19. "Roberta Alexander at Conference," *Black Panther*, 2 August 1969, 7.

20. Heath, *Off the Pigs*, 344.

21. Ibid.

22. Belva Butcher, interview with author, 8 October 1990, Oakland, Calif., updated 13 September 2002; Kiilu Nyasha, interview with author, 27 October 1990; *Black Panthers: Voices of Panther Women*.

23. Lu Hudson, interview with author, October 7, 2002.

24. Ibid.

25. Ibid.

26. Lu Hudson resignation letter, 20 February 1979, Huey Newton Foundation Collection, series 2, subseries 2, box 4, folder 19.

27. Hudson, interview.

28. Ibid.

29. Angela D. LeBlanc-Ernest, "The Most Qualified Person to Handle the Job: Black Panther Party Women, 1966–1982," in *Black Panther Party Reconsidered*, 324–25; JoNina Abron, letter to Karen Edgecombe, giving her dates of service and discussing other business, 15 April 1981, Abron Papers.

30. Abron, "Comrade Sisters' Relationship Outside the Party," 10 August 1977, Huey Newton Foundation Collection, series 2, subseries 2, box 4, folder 19.

31. Ibid.

32. Ibid.

33. "Dale," "Women in the Perty" [*sic*], 4 October 1977, Huey Newton Foundation Collection, series 2, subseries 2, box 4, folder 19.

34. Hudson, interview.

35. Hudson, interview; Brown, "Servants of the People," 67.

36. LeBlanc-Ernest, "Most Qualified Person," 319–20; Seale states that Jones wants to dis-

cuss birth control policies in Comrade Bobby, "All Comrades of the Central Body" memo, 16 August 1972, Huey Newton Foundation Collection, series 2, subseries 2, box 4, folder 2.

37. "Directive" from Huey Newton, 14 January 1974, Huey Newton Foundation Collection, series 2, subseries 2, box 4, folder 14.

38. Tommye Williams, memo to Huey Newton, undated, Huey Newton Foundation Collection, series 2, subseries 2, box 4, folder 19.

39. Brown, "Servants of the People," 85–86.

40. Brown, *Taste of Power*, 189; Tracye Matthews, "No One Ever Asks What a Man's Place in the Revolution Is: Gender and the Politics of the BPP, 1966–1971," in *Black Panther Party Reconsidered*, 281.

41. "Black Panther Revolutionary Wedding," *Black Panther*, 11 May 1969, 7.

42. "Revolutionary Marriage," *Black Panther*, 28 June 1969, 17.

43. "A Wedding of Revolutionaries," *Black Panther*, 23 August 1969, 13.

44. "Revolutionary Love, Revolutionary Wedding," *Black Panther*, 30 August 1969, 14.

45. Hilliard and Cole, *This Side of Glory*, 221–23, 251–52, 300–301, 315–16; Brown, *Taste of Power*, 259–60. Hilliard discusses his wife's negative reaction to his mistress and how she later slept with Newton, which in turn caused Hilliard to be jealous. Brown felt pangs of envy and jealousy when Newton had encounters with other women; correspondence regarding the expulsion of David and June Hilliard, 1974, Huey Newton Foundation Collection, series 2, subseries 1, box 1, folder 6.

46. Shakur, *Assata*, 223–25.

47. Brown, "Servants of the People," 66–67. A female party member narrates an incident where a male Panther attempted to use his authority to coerce a sexual relationship.

Chapter 6

The epigraph to this chapter is from "The Story of the Black Panther Party: From Revolution to Evolution," *African Mirror*, August 1980, 45, Abron Papers.

1. "Seale Explains Increased Programs to Aid Black Community Survival," *Stanford Daily*, 23 November 1971, n.p., Huey Newton Foundation Collection, series 8, box 4, folder 4.

2. "Panthers Turn to Pork Chop Politics," *San Francisco Examiner*, 9 March 1972, 22, Huey P. Newton Foundation Collection, series 8, box 4, folder 4; "Chairman Bobby for Mayor!" *Black Panther*, 20 May 1972, suppl., A–D.

3. "Eldridge Cleaver for President, Kathleen Cleaver for Assemblywoman 18th District, Huey Newton for 7th District Congress, Bobby Seale for State Assemblyman 17th District," *Black Panther*, 18 May 1968, 17–19.

4. Johnson, "Explaining the Demise," 403–6.

5. Donald Mosby, "Panthers Emerging Out of the Ashes of Tragedy, Despair," *Muhammad Speaks*, 16 March 1973, 30.

6. "Seale in Mayor Runoff: Vicious Fight Seen," *Berkeley Barb*, 20–26 April 1973, 5.

7. B. J. Mason, "A Shift to the Middle: Chairman Bobby Seale Changes Black Panther Image to Fit the Times," *Ebony*, August 1973, 80–87.

8. "Campaign Upsets Politics As Usual Game," *Berkeley Barb*, 23–29 March 1973, 6.

9. "Bobby Seale Calls upon Oakland City Council to Become the First City in Cali-

fornia to Provide Bilingual (English/Spanish) Ballots for Local Elections," BPP campaign flyer; "Why Gay People Should Vote for Bobby Seale and Elaine Brown," Alice B. Toklas Memorial Democratic Club flyer, Huey P. Newton Foundation Collection, series 2, subseries 7, box 45, folder 19; "Gays Will Back Bobby, Elaine," *Berkeley Barb*, 6–12 April 1973, 10.

10. City of Oakland Election Returns, Municipal Nominating and General Election, April 17 and May 15, 1973, 97, Oakland City Clerk's Office; "Seale Puts Oakland into Runoff," *New York Times*, 19 April 1973, 27; "Bobby's Backers Look for Win," *Berkeley Barb* 17 May 1973, 8.

11. City of Oakland Election Returns, Municipal and General Election, April 17 and May 15, 1973, 98; "Bobby Seale Still Running," *San Francisco Chronicle*, 17 May 1973, 4; "Bobby Elated over Future Despite Loss," *Berkeley Barb*, 18 May 1973, 10.

12. Bobby Seale, memo dated 6 March 1974, to all central body members regarding whether he should join the NAACP and the party's relationship to the Black Political Convention in Little Rock, Arkansas, March 15–17, 1974; James T. Toliver, Jr., letter to Bobby Seale requesting that Seale join the Bay Area Urban League, 14 March 1974, Huey P. Newton Foundation Collection, series 2, subseries 2, box 4, folder 3.

13. "Black Political Agenda," January 1974, Huey Newton Foundation Collection, series 2, subseries 2, box 4, folder 4.

14. Brown, *Taste of Power*, 347–52.

15. "College Teacher Beaten in Class," *San Francisco Chronicle*, 16 November 1972, 3.

16. "Behind an Ugly Incident at Peralta College," *San Francisco Examiner*, 6 December 1972, 8; "Fritz and Huey: We're Not Enemies," *Grove Street Grapevine*, 7 December 1972, 1, Huey Newton Foundation Collection, series 8, box 2, folder 1.

17. "Behind an Ugly Incident"; "Fritz and Huey."

18. Seale, *Seize the Time,* 113–32.

19. "Hilliard Falls from Grace," *Bay Guardian*, 27 April 1974, 3, Johnson, "Explaining the Demise," 406–9; Brown, *Taste of Power*, 347–52; "Panther Newton Is Arrested," *San Francisco Chronicle*, 31 July 1974, n.p.; Pearl Stewart, "Black Panther Party Falters," *Oakland Tribune*, 27 November 1977, 2C; "Huey Newton Found Shot to Death," *San Francisco Examiner*, 22 August 1989, A-1.

20. Bob Lucas, "East Oakland Ghetto Blooms with Growth of Black Panther School, *Jet Magazine*, 5 February 1976, Huey P. Newton Foundation Collection, series 2, subseries 3, box 16, folder 2.

21. "Black Panther on Board," *Oakland Tribune*, 14 May 1976, 3; Michael Ackley, "Blacks, Poor Win Voice on School Board," *Montclarion*, 12 May 1976, n.p., Huey P. Newton Foundation Collection, series 2, subseries 3, box 16, folder 2.

22. "The World Is Their Classroom: Interview with Ms. Brenda Bay, Director of Intercommunal Youth Institute," *Black Panther*, 3 November 1973, 4; "Chicago Model Cities Election—December 19th People's Candidates Campaign for Public Office," *Black Panther* 7 December 1972, 6.

23. Huey P. Newton, "On the Relevance of the Church," *Huey P. Newton Reader*, 214–

24. Ephesians 6:5, *New International Version of the Holy Bible* (Grand Rapids, Mich.: Zondervan Publishing, 1984).

25. Earl Neal, "Hallelujah! The People's Revolutionary Gospel," *Black Panther*, 18 December 1971, 10.

26. "The Role of the Church and the Survival Program," *Black Panther*, 15 May 1971, 10–12; "Revival for Survival: Save Bobby and Erika, Save Black People," *Black Panther*, 15 May 1971, 13.

27. "Son of Man Temple: Statement of Purpose," *Black Panther*, 17 November 1973, 4; pamphlet, 2 September 1973, from Son of Man Temple featuring People's Free Medical Research Health Clinics; pamphlet, 16 September 1973, from Son of Man Temple featuring David Hilliard People's Free Shoe Program; pamphlet, n.d., from Son of Man Temple announcing that Dr. Henry Bryant, black studies instructor from Laney College, and Will St. Young from Grove Street College will make presentations on 28 April 1974; flyer from Son of Man Temple announcing David Sibeko from the Pan-Africanist Congress and David Du-Bois (editor of *Black Panther*) will speak on "Black People and the Mideast Conflict" on 28 October 1973; all from Huey Newton Foundation Collection, series 2, box 18.

28. Huey P. Newton, "On the Relevance of the Church," speech delivered 19 May 1971 at the Center for Urban Black Studies, Graduate Theological Union, Berkeley, California, Huey Newton Foundation Collection, series 2, subseries 3, box 18, folder 10; quiz on the history of the black church, the development of black businesses and black capitalism reanalyzed, and the history of the Black Panther Party, 1973 review quiz no. 2, Huey P. Newton Foundation Collection, series 2, subseries 2, central committee information, box 4, folder 3.

29. George Williamson, "Police Tell Theory of Black Panther 'Purge,'" *San Francisco Chronicle*, 8 December 1977, 1; Abron Papers.

30. Pearl Stewart "Two Suspects in Panther Shooting Get City Pay," *Oakland Tribune*, 3 November 1977, 1; Abron Papers.

31. "Panther Leader Resigns," *Oakland Tribune*, 22 November 1977; Tim Reiterman, "Panther Leader Brown Resigns," *San Francisco Examiner*, 22 November 1977, 3; Pearl Stewart, "Mayor Resigns EOC Post," *Oakland Tribune*, 1 November 1977, 1; Lance Williams and Pearl Stewart, "Panthers' School Chief Sued," *Oakland Tribune*, 10 November 1977, 1; Rick Malaspina, "Audit of Funds to Panthers," *Oakland Tribune*, 22 November 1977, 1; Abron Papers; statement of Elaine Brown regarding the Black Panther Party, 16 November 1977, Huey P. Newton Foundation Collection, series 2, subseries 7, box 41, folder 12; "Huey Newton Found Shot to Death," *San Francisco Examiner*, 22 August 1989, 1.

32. "Party Members (as of Feb. 15, 1979)—total number 58," Huey Newton Foundation Collection, series 2, subseries 2, box 4, folder 6; Abron, memo to Huey P. Newton regarding the direction of the party, 1 October 1980, Huey P. Collection, series 2, subseries 2, box 4, folder 12.

33. "Party Members (as of Feb. 15, 1979)"; Abron, memo to Newton.

34. Unsigned memo to Newton, 1 May 1979, Huey P. Collection, series 2, subseries 2, box 4, folder 19. Abron's memo and this one are very frank in assessing the BPP's dim prospects in the future.

Epilogue

The epigraph to this section is from Shakur, *Assata,* 243.

1. "Nationwide Harassment of Panthers by Pig Power Structure," Pigs Raid Des Moines Panthers," "Indianapolis Panthers Target of Pig Attack," "Pigs Uptight: Bomb NJ Panther Office," *Black Panther*, 15 January 1969, 8–9; "Boston Panthers Maced and Beaten for Sell-

ing Panther Newspapers," *Black Panther*, 28 June 1969, 16; "Press Conference: Pigs Attack Toledo NCCF," *Black Panther*, 3 October 1970, 4. These articles and many others appeared on a regular basis from 1967–1973 in the party newspaper.

2. Carmichael and Hamilton, *Black Power*, 172–73.

3. Black Panther Party, *Fallen Comrades*. The BPP listed twenty-seven members who died by violent means. Only one death, that of Cindy Smallwood, could be classified as normal. Smallwood died in a 1973 traffic accident.

4. Haley, *Autobiography of Malcolm X*, 345.

5. Tyson, *Radio Free Dixie*, 300–305.

6. "Chairman Bobby Seale," 11.

7. Eugene Williams, interview; Robertson, interview; Shakur, *Assata*, 221–22.

8. Maurice C. Cornforth, *Materialism and the Dialectical Method* (New York: International Publishers, 1971). This text was first published in London in 1952 and is a basic primer on the concept of dialectical materialism; Bobby Seale, Ericka Huggins, and Michael Cross, "Political Education and the Renewal of the Ideological Institute," memo to the central body, 28 August 1973, Huey Newton Foundation Collection, series 2, subseries 2, box 4, folder 3. Seale and the others acknowledge the low educational level of the membership and recommend dividing the classes into higher and lower levels.

BIBLIOGRAPHIC ESSAY

The *Black Panther Black Community News Service* is the most important primary source for the ideology and actions of the Black Panther Party. The *Black Panther*'s first issue was in April 1967, but publication was sporadic until it became a weekly in January 1968. The name was changed to the *Black Panther Intercommunal News Service* after February 1971.

Eldridge Cleaver was the first editor, and his militant influence was felt long after he went into exile. Andrew Austin, Elbert "Big Man" Howard, and JoNina Abron were also editors of the *Black Panther*. Provocative language, an imaginative and artistic layout, and biting cartoons drawn by BPP minister of culture Emory Douglas (and other graphic artists) increased the newspaper's popularity. The *Black Panther* established a reputation for fiery rhetoric, which lasted from 1967 until approximately 1972, when the BPP adopted a more moderate attitude in print as well as in action.

J. Edgar Hoover considered the newspaper the most effective BPP public relations effort. Hoover claimed that its weekly circulation was in excess of 100,000 by 1970 and occasionally reached 139,000. The FBI engaged in numerous schemes to interfere with the publication and distribution of the paper as part of its counterintelligence operations.[1] Weekly publication continued through 1978, when financial difficulties forced a more sporadic schedule. Publication ceased altogether in 1980.

The Panther Party also issued a stream of pamphlets that commented on important ideological and cultural issues. *Fallen Comrades of the Black Panther Party* narrates the BPP version of how and why their casualties occurred. Eldridge Cleaver's pamphlets *On the Ideology of the Black Panther Party* and *Land Question and Black Liberation* were originally published as a series of newspaper articles before he fell out of favor. The writings demonstrate Cleaver's role in forming Panther ideology.

Michael "Cetewayo" Tabor's 1969 pamphlet *Capitalism Plus Dope Equals Genocide* was written when he was a New York 21 prisoner. Tabor, a former heroin addict, explains the Panther Party's position on the nature of the drug epidemic plaguing the black community.

Different offices also issued regional newsletters and papers. The Los Angeles chapter's *Southern California Spark*, the Rockford (Ill.) branch's *Newsletter*, and the Illinois state chapter's *Ministry of Information Bulletin* are examples of these regional communications. These materials would supplement the regular party newspaper. They also demonstrate the particular characteristics and strengths of regional organizing efforts. They are invaluable for further insight into local Panther politics and personalities. I would like to thank Dr. William Burr for generously allowing me to copy his original issues from the Chicago and Rockford branches of the Illinois BPP chapter. Dr. Burr is an analyst with George Washington University's national security archive.

From 1971 to 1974 the East Coast faction of the BPP "split" published a newspaper called *Right On!* The first issue had several articles that critique the ideological and ethical position of the Newton wing of the BPP. *Right On!* is absolutely necessary to understanding the Panther schism and why a rival organization was set up in New Jersey and New York. Amherst College Marshall Bloom Underground Newspaper Collection and the Wisconsin State Historical Society have copies. Researchers should, of course, supplement these highly partisan journals with other contemporary sources to obtain a more balanced account of Panther activities.

Contemporary news accounts (establishment and underground) of the BPP's activities provide another analysis of Panther activity. Earl Caldwell was one of the more knowledgeable observers of the BPP during the 1960s and

1970s. Caldwell's March 1, 1971, *New York Times* material on the Panther schism offers an informed and balanced perspective.

On October 14, 1970, the *New Orleans Times-Picayune* began a series of articles by Georgie Anne Geyer and Keyes Beech on Cuba's relations with American radicals. Geyer and Beech interviewed Robert F. Williams after his return from overseas. Williams discusses the BPP's relations with the Cuban government. In addition there are allegations that Cuba provided guerilla training to American blacks, including Panthers.

Williams's allegations were buttressed decades later when the *Memphis Commercial-Appeal* began publishing a March 1993 series about domestic spying by U.S. military intelligence. The March 21 and March 22 stories also discuss Cuban training of black American radicals. These newspaper reports are very important for researchers interested in this matter.

Seymour Hersh's March 17, 1978, article in the *New York Times* examines little-known foreign intelligence operations designed to subvert the BPP. Historians should also be aware that various reporters on establishment papers might have served as conduits for law enforcement leaks designed to put a favorable police slant on a seemingly straight news story. The FBI referred to these reporters as public or open sources. Articles by reporters who worked the police beat should be read with this possibility in mind. This awareness will allow for a proper assessment of press sources for credibility and spin because the counterintelligence program relied on reporters for misinformation intended to intimidate or mislead the radical community about the surveillance to which it was subjected.

Underground press accounts in the *Los Angeles Free Press*, the *Berkeley Barb*, the *Berkeley Tribe*, and New York's *East Village Other* offer counterculture views on the BPP and other contemporary politics. There were, of course, many of these publications throughout the country. Researchers should determine which ones were active in their regions.

The United States government issued a variety of reports relating to the Panthers. The House of Representatives' Internal Security Committee published *The Black Panther Party, Its Origin and Development as Reflected in Its Official Weekly Newspaper: The Black Panther Black Community News Service* (1970) and *Gun-Barrel Politics: The Black Panther Party, 1966–1971* (1971). These sources are very thorough and demonstrate that the government responded to the party's revolutionary rhetoric and was not influenced to halt or change its tactics by the survival programs. In other words, in addition to its own inclinations, the government used the party's publications to justify action against a perceived threat to internal security.

The U.S. Senate Intelligence Committee published *Book 3: Final Report of the Select Committee to Study Government Operations with Respect to Intelligence Operations* (1976). The report covers domestic and international operations against the BPP and supplies details that are not in some FBI memos. These documents contain a wealth of information about certain aspects of government operations and are a rewarding source for the historian.

Other government reports, such as the 1970 U.S. census, provide valuable demographic information on the educational and social characteristics of the Panther recruitment pool. The 1973 City of Oakland election returns and precinct maps also aid in understanding the Seale-Huggins electoral campaign.

The Counter-Intelligence Program of the FBI, available from Scholarly Resources of Wilmington, Delaware, is a microfilm collection of Department of Justice files on a variety of political groups: Communists, socialists, white racist groups, and Black Nationalist organizations.[2] The FBI's counterintelligence program's memos on the Panther Party are catalogued under Black Nationalist hate groups. Though the memos are supposedly filed chronologically by month and year, some are out of sequence. For example, a September 1967 memo might be found in the second week of April 1968. Researchers attempting to follow a paper trail should be aware of this anomaly.

FBI agents speak frankly in these memos about infiltration, recruitment methods, and rumors making the rounds within the BPP. Operational tactics are assessed, and suggestions are given for adding to the BPP's inner turmoil. The memos also include letters, newspaper clippings, and examples of the cartoons and other "poison pen" material mailed to the Panthers.

Party members, of course, have produced many primary materials. Bobby Seale's *Seize the Time: The Story of the Black Panther Party and Huey P. Newton* (1970), the New York 21's *Look for Me in the Whirlwind: The Collective Autobiography of the New York 21* (1971), and Assata Shakur's *Assata: An Autobiography* (1987) were written as events were unfolding.

These autobiographies are a key indicator of the Panthers' worldview. Seale book documents the party's founding and early ideological influences. It was written to build support for the organization and justify Panther politics and tactics. Consequently, Seale goes into great detail about the reasons for basing early organizing efforts on the "brothers on the block" and Malcolm X's influence on the Panthers.

The New York 21 and Assata Shakur describe the growing political consciousness among young blacks that led them to the BPP. Their accounts are valuable because they cover the experiences of rank-and-file-members. Shakur also played an important role in the BLA underground before escaping from prison and going into exile in Cuba. Shakur's autobiography aids in understanding how ordinary people were led almost imperceptibly into the life of an urban guerilla.

Shakur and her colleagues believed they were following scientific revolutionary principles. They fully expected that the majority of black Americans would publicly endorse and support their actions. The militants were frustrated and disappointed when the anticipated uprising did not happen. The collapse of the "revolution" forced them to the unwelcome realization that they had misinterpreted the country's political mood and tendencies. Some former Panthers believe this misinterpretation might be the BPP's greatest failure because it led to a tragic loss of life and human potential for militants, police, and innocent families.

To Die for the People: The Writings of Huey P. Newton (1972), *Revolutionary Suicide* (1973), and Newton's doctoral dissertation, "War against the Panthers: A Study of Repression in America" (1996) attempt to justify Newton's political transformations. There is no thorough examination of any personal or organizational faults. These writings are collectively disappointing because of these shortcomings.

A year-by-year analysis of Newton's contemporary writings in the newspaper or other journals offers a more accurate insight into his contemporary thinking. For example, an August 1969 *Ebony* article written by Newton and titled "The Black Panthers" is an accurate reflection of the party's message. Newton's later writings demonstrate a concern with "clarifying" the historical record.

In the last ten years several new books have purported to reexamine the historical significance and meaning of the BPP. These texts fall into three broad categories. The first category consists of autobiographical efforts to narrate party history through the writer's personal engagement in Panther activity. These authors offer an insider's view of the party's internal and external struggles and tend toward the sensational in revealing personal shortcomings and peccadilloes.

Elaine Brown's *A Taste of Power: A Black Woman's Story* (1992) and David Hilliard and Lewis Cole's *This Side of Glory: The Autobiography of David Hilliard and the Story of the Black Panther Party* (1993) exemplify this category. Brown's work has also attempted to portray the influence of Panther women, primarily by citing herself as an example. Brown rose from the Los Angeles rank and file to become the minister of information after Cleaver's ouster. She became the party's leader during Newton's Cuban exile.

Hilliard, BPP chief of staff, was instrumental in organizing and leading the BPP during the incarceration of Newton and Seale. Both his story and Brown are valuable for their perspectives on Panther culture and the party's internal dynamics.

For example, each acknowledges the widespread use of physical discipline in the BPP and the existence of a party underground. Both accounts, however, suffer from an overemphasis on personal foibles and sexual adventures at the expense of a strictly political analysis of the Panther Party.

Hugh Pearson's text, *The Shadow of the Panther: Huey Newton and Price of Black Power in America* (1984), is in a category by itself. Pearson undertakes the task of chronicling party history through a narration of legal mishaps and antisocial activity. Consequently, Pearson lays too much stress on militarism and the well-known self-destructive attitudes of some party members in the later years. This approach prevents him from comprehending the importance of ideology and community action for the rank and file. In other words, the party's equally well-known political organizing does not receive proper attention. The BPP is a one-dimensional animal for Pearson.

Academia is the final category. My research indicates that Charles Hopkins was the first academic to write about the first Panther political transformation, which he covered in his 1978 Ph.D. dissertation, "The Deradicalization of the Black Panther Party: 1966–1973."[3] Hopkins demonstrated that over a seven-year period the BPP changed its political philosophy from overt calls to revolution to a more reform-oriented agenda.

Other theses and dissertations on different aspects of Panther history have been produced in the last fifteen years. Kit Kim Holder's 1990 Ph.D. dissertation is an excellent national history of the BPP from 1966 to 1972. Holder examines organizational structure, activities, political coalitions, leadership failures, and the government campaign to destroy the Panthers during their first ideological era. This excellent text demonstrates an intimate knowledge of the Panther Party and should encourage historians and social scientists to study the party as a serious political entity.[4]

Angela LeBlanc-Ernest, Robin Spencer, and Tracye Matthews have all analyzed the role of women in the BPP. Kathleen Cleaver, former communications secretary, wrote her senior thesis on the international branch's activities in Algeria. Charles E. Jones's *The Black Panther Party Reconsidered* (1998) and Kathleen Cleaver and George Katsiaficas's *Liberation, Imagination, and the Black Panther Party* (2001) are some of the more recent entries.[5] Both Jones's book and Cleaver and Katsiaficas's book consist of essays from former Panthers and scholars. The essays examine the role of women, organizational dynamics, ideology, international relations, survival programs, the *Black Panther*, political prisoners, the BLA, and the party's political legacy. These texts are also extremely useful as guides to excellent primary sources.

Many visual artists documented the BPP, and material is still being produced. For example, New York City's 2001 Second International Black Panther Film Festival assembled old and new film and videos for presentation. Some of the films were *The Murder of Fred Hampton* (1971), *Eyes of the Rainbow* (1997), *All Power to the People* (1996), and *Black Panther in Exile: The Pete O'Neal Story (A Work in Progress)* (1990). *The Murder of Fred Hampton* begins in 1968 and follows the twenty-one-year-old Panther leader through arrests and harassment as he oversees the extraordinary growth of the Chicago chapter. *Eyes of the Rainbow* is an interview with Assata Shakur, who has lived as an exile in Cuba for the past twenty years. *All Power to the People* interviews former Panthers Safiya Bukhari (now deceased), Bobby Seale, Kathleen Cleaver, and Richard "Dhoruba" Moore and former government officials as they attempt to answer what happened to the movement. *Black Panther in Exile* explores the Kansas City Panthers and Pete O'Neal's African exile.[6]

In 1990 the University of California's Graduate Assembly sponsored a forum on the historical legacy and political lessons of the BPP. The two-day event was filmed under the title *The Black Panthers: From Generation to Generation*. A videotape, *The Black Panthers: The Voices of Black Panther Women*, is part of the forum's panel discussion of rank-and-file Panthers relating their experiences and giving their reasons for joining the party. The tape is available at the University of California-Berkeley's Moffitt Library.

The BPP film library's most valuable assets are the oral interviews with the rank and file. Ordinary members are usually very frank in assessing the organization's successes and failures. They believe that they made a unique contribution to the civil rights movement and that that contribution should not be confused with the misdeeds of a few leaders. Rank-and-file Panthers are adamant that it was their work that kept the survival programs functioning, and they want their stories told. Their oral histories are invaluable in reconstructing the historical record.

Last, there are the current publications devoted to keeping the Panther Party's memory alive. *It's About Time* is an online publication produced by a Sacramento-based group of former Panthers and their supporters. The nonprofit organization publishes current news and covers the present activities of former Panthers. The newspaper staff maintains a speakers' bureau, provides mentoring to urban youth, organizes local community groups, and provides information to the public on issues of social justice. In 2002 the group sponsored a thirty-fifth reunion and conference of the Black Panther Party in Washington, D.C., and the first West Coast Black Panther Party Film Festival at Oakland's Laney College.

David Hilliard serves as a director of the Dr. Huey P. Newton Foundation, which develops and sponsors educational programs that maintain the BPP political philosophy. Perhaps the foundation is best known for providing the Black Panther archive to the Stanford University Libraries. The archive contains the BPP's internal records and correspondence, government documents, manuscripts, papers, photographs, art, and videotapes. It is a necessary and invaluable tool to any researcher working on party topics.

The Moorland-Spingarn Research Center at Howard University also has a Panther archive. Former members have contributed their personal papers, memorabilia, and photographs to the center. Many of these documents are from the BPP's later years of 1974 to 1982.

The Black Panther Newspaper Committee was composed of former Panthers, and it republished the *Black Panther* from 1991 to 1993 as a quarterly. The committee established distribution and news-gathering offices in Chicago, New York City, Jersey City, Kansas City, Oklahoma City, San Antonio, Long Beach, and Oakland.[7] There was a short period of time when the committee discussed the possibility of reestablishing the BPP, but this never occurred, and the revitalized *Black Panther* also ceased publication in 1993. All of the above materials have attempted to maintain the BPP's ideology and historical memory. They are extremely helpful in determining what former members are involved in today and how to contact them for information on past and present activities.

This is by no means a complete bibliography of sources and archives. Some former Panthers and private collectors have their own repositories of material. These papers will, I hope, make their way into the public eye as the years go on. The BPP's history, like all history, is a constantly evolving narrative, one that will reveal more and more facts as time goes on.

Notes

1. U.S. Senate, Committee to Study Government Operations, *Book 3: Final Report of the Select Committee to Study Government Operations with Respect to Intelligence,* 94th Cong., 2nd sess. (Washington, D.C.: Government Printing Office, 1976), 214.

2. *The Counter-Intelligence Program of the FBI* (Wilmington, Del.: Scholarly Resources, 1978).

3. Charles William Hopkins, "The Deradicalization of the Black Panther Party: 1966–1973" (Ph.D. diss., University of North Carolina at Chapel Hill, 1978).

4. Kit Kim Holder, "The History of the Black Panther Party, 1966–1972" (Ph.D. diss., University of Massachusetts, 1990).

5. Kathleen Cleaver, "The Evolution of the International Section of the Black Panther Party in Algiers, 1969–1972" (senior essay, Yale University, 9 December 1983); Angela Darlean Brown, "Servants of the People: A History of Women in the Black Panther Party" (senior honors thesis, Harvard University, 23 March 1992); Tracye A. Matthews, "No One Ever Asks What a Man's Role in the Revolution Is: Gender and Sexual Politics in the Black Panther Party, 1966–1971" (Ph.D. diss., University of Michigan, 1998); Robyn Spencer, "Repression Breeds Resistance: The Rise and Fall of the Black Panther Party in Oakland, California, 1966–1982" (Ph.D. diss., Columbia University, 2001); Charles E. Jones, ed., *The Black Panthers Reconsidered* (Baltimore: Black Classic Press, 1998); Kathleen Cleaver and George Katsiaficas, *Liberation, Imagination, and the Black Panther Party: A New Look at the Panthers and Their Legacy* (New York: Routledge, 2001).

6. Pamphlet, Second International Black Panther Film Festival, New York, 2001.

7. Bill O'Brien, "The Return of the Black Panther," *East Bay Express,* 19 April 1991, 3.

SELECTED BIBLIOGRAPHY

Archives

Black Panther Party Archives, Moorland-Spingarn Research Center, Howard University, Washington, D.C.

Bloom Alternative Press Collection, Amherst College Archives and Special Collections, Amherst, Mass.

Walter Loving Papers, Moorland-Spingarn Research Center, Howard University, Washington, D.C.

Huey P. Newton Foundation Collection, Department of Special Collections, Stanford University Libraries, Palo Alto, Calif.

University of California-Berkeley, Bancroft Library, Berkeley, Calif.

Wisconsin State Historical Society, Madison, Wis.

Books, Pamphlets, Periodicals, and Audiovisual Materials

"Algeria: Panthers on Ice." *Time*, 4 September 1972, 32.

Black Panther Party. *Fallen Comrades of the Black Panther Party.* Oakland, Calif.: Black Panther Party, 1973.

The Black Panthers: Voices of Black Panther Women. Videotape. Berkeley, Calif.: Media Resources Center, 26 October 1990.

Black Power, Black Panthers. San Francisco: KQED, 1990.

Brown, Elaine. *A Taste of Power: A Black Woman's Story.* New York: Pantheon Books, 1992.

Carmichael, Stokely, and Charles V. Hamilton. *Black Power: The Politics of Liberation in America.* New York: Vintage Books, 1967.

Carmichael, Stokely, and Michael Thelwell. *Ready for Revolution: The Life and Struggles of Stokely Carmichael (Kwame Ture).* New York: Scribner, 2005.

Cleaver, Eldridge. *On the Ideology of the Black Panther Party.* Oakland, Calif.: Black Panther Party, 1968.

———. *Soul on Ice.* New York: Delta, 1968.

Cleaver, Kathleen, and George Katsiaficas, eds. *Liberation, Imagination, and the Black Panther Party: A New Look at the Panthers and Their Legacy.* New York: Routledge, 2001.

Clegg, Claude Andrew, III. *An Original Man: The Life and Times of Elijah Muhammad.* New York: St. Martin's Press, 1997.

Cornforth, Maurice. *Materialism and the Dialectical Method.* New York: International Publishers, 1971.

Cruse, Harold. *The Crisis of the Negro Intellectual: From Its Origins to the Present.* New York: William Morrow and Co., 1967.

DuBois, W. E. B. *Dusk of Dawn: An Essay toward an Autobiography of a Race Concept.* New York: Harcourt, Brace, and Co., 1940.

Dudziak, Mary L. *Cold War Civil Rights: Race and the Image of American Democracy.* Princeton, N.J.: Princeton University Press, 2000.

Epstein, Edward Jay. "A Reporter at Large, the Panthers and the Police: A Pattern of Genocide?" *New Yorker,* 13 February 1971, 45–78.

Fanon, Frantz. *The Wretched of the Earth.* New York: Grove Press, 1963.

Gitlin, Todd. *The Sixties: Years of Hope, Days of Rage.* New York: Bantam Books, 1987.

Haley, Alex. *The Autobiography of Malcolm X.* New York: Grove Press, 1965.

Heath, Louis, ed. *The Black Panthers Speak: Huey P. Newton, Bobby Seale, Eldridge Cleaver and Company Speak Out through the Black Panther Party's Official Newspaper.* Metuchen, N.J.: Scarecrow Press, 1976.

———. *The History and Literature of the Black Panther Party.* Metuchen, N.J.: Scarecrow Press, 1976.

Henry, Imani. "Black Liberation Army Soldier Speaks." *Worker's World News Service,* 1 September 2002.

Hilliard, David, and Lewis Cole. *This Side of Glory: The Autobiography of David Hilliard and the Story of the Black Panther Party.* Boston: Little, Brown, and Co., 1993.

Hilliard, David, and Donald Weise, eds. *The Huey P. Newton Reader.* New York: Seven Stories Press, 2002.

Jackson, George. *Blood in My Eye.* Baltimore: Black Classic Press, 1990.

Jones, Charles E., ed. *The Black Panther Party Reconsidered.* Baltimore: Black Classic Press, 1998.

Karim, Benjamin, ed. *The End of White World Supremacy: Four Speeches by Malcolm X.* New York: Arcade Publishing, 1971.

Knapper, Karl. "Women and the Black Panther Party: An Interview with Angela Brown." *Socialist Review* 26, nos. 1 and 2 (1996): 34–66.

Lewis, David Levering. *W. E. B. DuBois: Biography of a Race.* New York: Henry Holt and Co., 1993.

Lincoln, C. Eric. *The Black Muslims in America.* Boston: Beacon Press, 1961.

Lucas, Bob. "East Oakland Ghetto Blooms with Growth of Black Panther School." *Jet,* 5 February 1976.

Malcolm X. *Grass Roots Speech: Detroit, Michigan, November 10, 1963.* New York: Paul Winley Records, 1963.

———. *Ballots or Bullets.* Detroit: First Amendment Records, 1964.

Marighela, Carlos. *Minimanual of the Urban Guerilla.* Havana: Tricontinental Press, 1969.

Mason, B. J. "A Shift to the Middle: Chairman Bobby Seale Changes Black Panther Image to Fit the Times." *Ebony,* August 1973, 80–87.

Muhammad, Elijah. *Message to the Blackman in America.* Chicago: Nation of Islam, 1965.

Newton, Huey. "The Black Panthers." *Ebony,* August 1969, 106–12.

———. *Revolutionary Suicide.* New York: Harcourt Brace Jovanovich, 1973. Reprint, New York: Writer's and Reader's Publishing, 1995.

———. *To Die for the People: The Writings of Huey P. Newton.* Edited by Franz Schurman. New York: Random House, 1972.

———. *War against the Panthers: A Study of Repression in America.* New York: Harlem River Press, 1996.

New York 21. *Look for Me in the Whirlwind: The Collective Autobiography of the New York 21.* New York: Vintage Books, 1971.

"The Panthers: Their Decline and Fall?" *Newsweek,* 22 March 1971, 26.

Perry, Bruce, ed. *Malcolm X: The Last Speeches.* New York: Pathfinder Press, 1989.

"Radicals: Destroying the Panther Myth." *Time,* 22 March 1971, 19.

Seale, Bobby. *A Lonely Rage: The Autobiography of Bobby Seale.* New York: Times Books, 1978.

———. *Seize the Time: The Story of the Black Panther Party and Huey P. Newton.* New York: Vintage Books, 1970.

Shabazz, Malcolm X. *Malcolm X at Berkeley.* Berkeley, Calif.: University of California Television Studio Archives, 11 October 1963.

Shakur, Assata. *Assata: An Autobiography.* Westport, Conn.: Lawrence Hill and Co., 1987.

"The Story of the Black Panther Party: From Revolution to Evolution." *African Mirror,* August 1980, 36–47.

Tabor, Michael "Cetewayo." *Capitalism Plus Dope Equals Genocide.* New York: Black Panther Party, 1970.

Theoharris, Jeanne F., and Komozi Woodward. *Freedom North: Black Freedom Struggles Outside the South, 1940–1980.* New York: Palgrave, 2003.

Tyson, Timothy B. *Radio Free Dixie: Robert F. Williams and the Roots of Black Power.* Chapel Hill: University of North Carolina Press, 1999.

Walton, Sidney F., Jr. *The Black Curriculum: Developing a Program in Afro-American Studies.* East Palo Alto, Calif.: Black Liberation Publishers, 1969.

Williams, Robert F. *Negroes with Guns.* Detroit: Wayne State University Press, 1998.

Williams, Yohuru. *Black Politics/White Power: Civil Rights, Black Power, and the Black Panthers in New Haven.* St. James, N.Y.: Brandywine Press, 2000.

Wolfe, Tom. *Radical Chic and Mau-Mauing the Flak Catchers.* New York: Farrar, Straus, and Giroux, 1970.

Wright, Thomas. "Who Fingered Carl Hampton?" *Sepia,* November 1970, 8–13.

Dissertations and Theses

Brown, Angela Darlean. "Servants of the People: A History of Women in the Black Panther Party." Senior honors thesis, Harvard University, 1992.

Holder, Kit Kim. "The History of the Black Panther Party, 1966–1972." Ph.D.diss., University of Massachusetts, 1990.

Hopkins, Charles William. "The Deradicalization of the Black Panther Party: 1966–1973. Ph.D. diss., University of North Carolina at Chapel Hill, 1978.

Matthews, Tracye A. "No One Ever Asks What a Man's Role in the Revolution Is: Gender and Sexual Politics in the Black Panther Party, 1966–1971." Ph.D. diss., University of Michigan, 1998.

Spencer, Robyn C. "Repression Breeds Resistance: The Rise and Fall of the Black Panther Party in Oakland, California, 1966–1982." Ph.D. diss., Columbia University, 2001.

Government Reports and Documents

City of Oakland Election Returns. Municipal Nominating and General Election: April 17 and May 15, 1973. Council districts by precinct. City Clerk's Office, Oakland, Calif.

The Counter-Intelligence Program of the FBI. Wilmington, Del.: Scholarly Resources, 1978. Thirty Reels.

U.S. Census, 1970. California Abstracts. General and Social Characteristics of the Negro Population. Washington, D.C.: U.S. Department of Commerce.

U.S. Congress. House of Representatives. Committee on Internal Security. *Gun-Barrel Politics: The Black Panther Party, 1966–1971.* 92nd Cong., 1st sess. Washington, D.C.: Government Printing Office, 1971.

U.S. Congress. Senate. Committee to Study Government Operations. *Book 3: Final Report of the Select Committee to Study Government Operations with Respect to Intelligence Operations.* 94th Cong., 2nd sess. Washington, D.C.: Government Printing Office, 1976.

INDEX